THE LOVER
&
THE SERPENT

Dreamwork within a
Sufi Tradition

LLEWELLYN VAUGHAN-LEE

FOREWORD BY
IRINA TWEEDIE

ELEMENT BOOKS

First published in Great Britain in 1990 by
Element Books Limited
Longmead, Shaftesbury, Dorset

Designed by Roger Lightfoot
Cover design by Max Fairbrother
Front cover illustration 'Birthstone' by
Deborah Koff-Chapin, from *At the Pool of Wonder*
© 1989 by Marcia Lauck and Deborah Koff-Chapin,
with permission of Bear & Company Publishing
Typeset by Photoprint, Torquay, Devon
Printed and bound in Great Britain by
Billings, Hylton Road, Worcester

British Library Cataloguing in Publication Data
Vaughan-Lee, Llewellyn
The lover & the serpent : dreamwork
within a Sufi tradition.
1. Sufism
I. Title
297.420

ISBN 1–85230–147–3

The wild geese do not intend to cast their reflection,
The water has no mind to receive their image.

CONTENTS

ACKNOWLEDGMENTS

For permission to use copyright material, the author gratefully wishes to acknowledge:
Blue Dolphin Publishing, for permission to quote from *Daughter of Fire*, by Irina Tweedie; Faber and Faber & Harcourt Brace Jovanovich, for permission to quote from 'Burnt Norton' and 'Little Gidding' in *The Four Quartets* by T.S. Eliot; Gower Publishing Group for permission to quote from *Tao Te Ching* translated by Gia–Fu Feng and Jane English; Khaniqahi–Nimatulla Publications, for permission to quote from *Sufi Symbolism, Volume 1* by Dr Javad Nurbakhsh; Phanes Press, for permission to quote from *The Drunken Universe* by Peter Lamborn Wilson and Nasrollah Pourjavady; Threshold Books, (RD 4 Box 600, Putney, VT 05346, USA) for permission to quote from *Open Secret* by John Moyne and Coleman Barks, and *Doorkeeper of the Heart* by Charles Upton; extract taken from *Rumi Poet and Mystic* by R.A. Nicholson reproduced by kind permission of Unwin Hyman Ltd.

PREFACE

I would like to thank all those whose dreams form the *prima materia* of this book.

Throughout this book God, the Great Beloved, is referred to as He. This is merely for the sake of convenience. The Absolute Truth is neither masculine nor feminine, though as much as It has a divine masculine side, so It has an awe-inspiring feminine aspect. Similarly, for the sake of convenience, the masculine pronoun is used predominantly for both the seeker and the Teacher.

FOREWORD

Every journey great or small begins with the first step, says a Chinese proverb. What leads the human being to make this inner journey in order to realise the Truth? 'Truth is God,' said Mahatma Gandhi. Sufis conceive God as 'Ultimate Reality', 'in which everything is and nothing is outside it'.

Each person will find his or her individual way and attract the circumstances for the inner development, which is very personal, very lonely and absolutely unique. There will be signposts on the way, but one must be ever alert to read the directions.

In each of us there is a strange and mysterious longing, a faint echo. We hear it and hear it not, and sometimes the whole life can pass without our knowing what this call is. I asked one of Bhai Sahib's disciples to translate a Persian song and it went like this:

> I am calling to you from afar
> Since aeons of time,
> Calling, calling, since always.
> I can't hear – so you say
> Who is calling and why?

Sometimes a very young child begins to ask questions about the meaning of life and the purpose of creation: 'Who is God? How did the world come about? Why am I here? Parents, *be* careful. Don't answer those questions glibly or facetiously. It may be, just may be, the first signpost. The first step leading us much later to the great inner journey.

Sometimes the death of someone we deeply love can force us to take the first step into the unknown. When faced with death in its mystery and horror we are obliged to look into our very depth. A sudden vision can be the very step, a near-

death experience, an accident – anything can cause it. But
more often than not it will be a dream, a specially meaningful
dream, perhaps a series of dreams, like windows opening
unexpectedly onto the vast, unexplored horizon.

Sufis believe in dreams. They hold them in great respect.
For our dreams arise in us from our very depths, from realms
in us of which our mind knows nothing. The human being
is ancient and deep and has no frontiers. Our substance is
part of the substance of the Great Being who contains
everything.

> And he to whom worshipping is a window, to open and to shut,
>   has not yet
> Visited the house of his soul whose windows are from dawn to
>   dawn.

> (Kahil Gibran, *The Prophet*)

Our consciousness can be as limitless as the Absolute or it
can be as tiny as a chicken's.

When I was writing my book, *Daughter of Fire*, how often
did I wonder how many people would understand what it
was all about, why did I do it, why did I strive and suffer
and fight with myself? Who would understand the burning
desire to be able to touch the outermost edges of conscious
awareness where, I dimly felt, must be hidden the secret
which leads to absolute freedom? Freedom from the bondage
which chains us to the wheel of life, of causation.

It is not easy to understand that the purpose of spiritual
training is to help the human being to control, to diminish
the ego. Our Teacher, Bhai Sahib, said, 'Two cannot live in
one heart. Make yourself empty; when your cup is empty
something else can fill it. But you people come to us, Sufis,
with your cup full *and* covered. How can I put anything into
it?'

The taming of the ego is a painful process. It is a crucifixion. One does not lose anything, or get rid of anything.
'You cannot become anything else but what you already are,'
said Carl Jung. We just learn to control our lower self and it
becomes our servant, not our master. The master is the Real
Us, our soul, and the real wisdom *is* in the soul.

In reading *The Lover and the Serpent: Dreamwork within a*

Sufi Tradition it was quite clear that Llewellyn caught the meaning, the subtle essence of spiritual training. He understood the pressing urge, that Something within the human heart, which drives the human being mercilessly on and on, no matter the sacrifice, sometimes with superhuman effort, to at least try to reach the ultimate Goal. Whatever that Goal may be for everyone of us.

Llewellyn came to our group very young. I think he was nineteen. He arrived wounded by life. His wings were clipped. Had his life much meaning? I don't think so. But he stayed and grew. He meditated. He worked upon himself. He watched, willing to surrender to his own Light. He persevered. And this is only the beginning.

We know how it begins, but we never know how it will end. It is the way leading into the infinite . . .

Llewellyn's study of Jungian psychology began with a dream in which he was told to read the works of Jung. At the moment he is lecturing extensively in the United States, and his approach to Sufism as seen from the modern psychological point of view is very original though closely fitting into the Sufi Tradition.

May our revered Teacher's Blessing be with him always and may my love be his companion on the Way.

I. Tweedie
London, June 1989

INTRODUCTION – THE
LOVER AND THE SERPENT

> A dream that is not understood remains a mere
> occurrence; understood it becomes a living experience
> (C. G. Jung).

Sufis are lovers of God. They are also travellers, making the
greatest of all journeys, the journey Home. This is a journey
that takes the Sufi into the depths of himself, into the
unknown inner world where the Beloved is to be found.
Dreams give the traveller guidance along this inner Path.
Speaking usually in the ancient language of images and
symbols, dreams are a source of great wisdom and insight.
This is true of the following dream, which was dreamt by a
woman soon after she came to a Sufi group.

> I am being kissed by a man. It is the most wonderful experience.
> It is not sexual, just a pure feeling of love in the heart. It touches
> me in the heart very deeply. But then I feel a tongue in my
> mouth, and it is not his tongue. I open my eyes and see that I
> am embracing a serpent, and it is the serpent's tongue in my
> mouth. I feel very frightened.

This dream contains two images that symbolise fundamental aspects of the Sufi Path, the lover and the serpent.
Sufism is a love affair, a relationship between the lover and
the Beloved. This is the core of all Sufi teaching, for it is in
the heart that Truth is to be found. Truth does not belong
to the mind but only to the heart; and love is that Truth made
manifest. God is love and the Path to Him ends in a lover's
embrace.

A love affair with the Great Beloved is no idealised
romance, but a passion that takes you into the very depths

of yourself, into the unknown places of your soul. A love affair with another human being will evoke previously unknown qualities of passion and feeling, reveal parts of yourself that you never knew before. If this is so with a human love affair, how much more will it be when He who is the King of Love touches your heart? The Great Beloved is a jealous Lover and He demands total commitment. He demands that the whole human being become involved, not just the personality but the very deepest, darkest parts. And the serpent, cold-blooded and instinctual, is an archetypal symbol for the deepest levels of the psyche, the primordial depths of which we have very little conscious awareness.

Thus this dream of the lover and the serpent describes how the great love affair, which is the essence of the Sufi Path, will take the dreamer into the very depths of herself, where she must embrace the serpent. Once she has accepted the serpent within, and loved that part of herself, then she will be able to love Him with the whole of herself. For,

How can you love somebody if you don't love yourself?
How can you give what you don't have?[1]

The Journey Home is a lover's return to the centre of himself, where He is waiting. And on this journey dreams are of immense importance, for it is through dreams that the inner world communicates to us, and guides us through its maze. The wisdom and understanding which we need for this quest lies within us, and it comes to us most easily in the form of dreams, when our conscious mind is asleep. Thus Sufis have always valued dreams and sought to understand the guidance which they offer.

This century has seen a reawakening of interest in the language of dreams, and dreamwork has been explored and developed from many differing psychological perspectives. However, little has been said about the relationship between dreams and specific spiritual traditions. For the last sixteen years I have attended a Sufi group in which dreamwork forms an integral part of the meetings and is the modern equivalent of the ancient Sufi teaching stories.

At the meetings of this Sufi group, individuals are encouraged to tell their dreams, which are then interpreted within the group. The dreamer benefits by sharing his/her dream and coming to understand its meaning. The very act of sharing a dream within a sympathetic group has immense psychological value, for then the unconscious of the dreamer knows that it is being listened to and appreciated. The psyche is highly sensitive and the attitude of the listener can be almost as important as that of the dreamer. When a dream is told the psyche reaches out from its inner world and its images cross the threshold into the light of day. The attitude of the listener can either dismiss or reinforce its imaginal reality, a reality that is so different to the concrete, material forms of the external world. Therefore, if the listener is receptive to the feeling quality and symbolic meaning of the dream, the psyche itself is valued:

> Through [the listener's] attitude he can affirm and recognise this product of the soul, thereby giving value and importance to the soul itself, to its creative, symbolic, awe-inspiring function. Is this not to bless the soul, for what a blessing this is for the psyche and its dream – and for the dreamer – to be affirmed and recognised in this way?[2]

When a dream is listened to without judgement or criticism, but with an openness of heart, a sympathetic soul, then the images of the dream are given substance. In this way the psyche and its symbolic forms are able to be more easily integrated into the conscious life of the dreamer.

The listeners also benefit. They share in the often-numinous quality of the dream. This is something that may in itself help them to appreciate their own symbolic reality. Just as fairy tales reassure children about the reality of their own symbolic perception of the world, in which monsters and princesses really exist, so too can another's dream echo within the listeners, evoking and speaking directly to their own psyche. Thus those who listen grow more familiar with the inner world of images, feel its magic, learn to understand and trust what it says.

But if the symbolic realm of the psyche is rarely appreciated within our rational culture, how much less is man's spiritual quest? How often does the world walk with hobnailed boots over this secret of the heart? Yet the Path Home, although the thinnest of golden threads, is the greatest of all dreams, indeed it is the underlying purpose of our whole existence. The spiritual call comes from deep within the psyche, and often it speaks to us in the language of dreams, guiding and instructing us along the Way. But spiritual dreams, dreams that point to the Empty Space beyond the horizon, have a particular quality of their own, and cannot be understood from a purely psychological perspective. One of the purposes of this book is to explore such dreams, and see how they can be best appreciated. But even if a spiritual dream is not consciously understood, when it is shared with friends in whose blood this invisible journey also sings, then there is a deep resonance as quest echoes quest. Within this resonance the dream can open like a flower and communicate its meaning from heart to heart. Here is one of the great values of a spiritual group: it provides an environment where the deepest longing of the heart can be heard, and its infinite wisdom listened to.

Sufi dreamwork is a group experience in which all participate. It is a sharing both by those who speak and those who remain silent. All learn about the spiritual path and the dynamics of the psyche as explored through the dream. Sufi dreamwork, which combines a spiritual and a psychological approach, presents a unique opportunity to understand the psychological processes encountered on the Path. At the meetings all are encouraged to offer interpretations. This presents the dreamer with a variety of perspectives on the dream, and gives the opportunity for others to develop their sensitivity and intuitive understanding of dreams. Sometimes the Teacher will suggest that one particular interpretation is correct, but more often it will be left for the dreamer to feel which of one or more interpretations are most appropriate. For, as with all dreamwork, the dreamer usually intuitively knows which is the right interpretation. Something 'clicks' as the conscious and the unconscious meet, and the psyche tells the dreamer that its message has been understood.

The dreamer will also often intuitively know when *not* to tell a dream. For some dreams are so intimate, are such a deep secret, that they are not to be told, but rather, like the shepherds' message to the Virgin Mary, 'kept, and pondered in the heart'. The dreamer may need to stay with the feeling, quality or symbolism of a dream and allow it to unfold itself slowly into his or her life, become part of his or her consciousness. Similarly, some dreams need to wait to be told, for, like seeds, they can germinate within the dreamer. If told too soon they may lose their numinous quality, or become contaminated by the ideas of others. But then, at the right moment, the dreamer feels an inner prompting to tell the dream. The dream suddenly comes to mind, possibly evoked by a dream told by someone else.

Not only does the unconscious know when it is right to share a dream, but it also appears to know whether there will be somebody present who can offer the correct interpretation of its symbolic message. On a number of occasions a dream will be told and there will happen to be someone present in the room who has come to the group just for that afternoon, and they will understand exactly what the dream means, perhaps having a particular knowledge of symbolism or an ancient language or culture that is referred to in the dream. This can be regarded as 'synchronicity' or meaningful coincidence; for in the psyche, time and space do not exist, and there, in the depths of ourselves, we are all one. We form part of what the ancients called the *anima mundi*, or world soul.

There is a marked difference between dreamwork as practised within this Sufi group and the usual analytic approach, in that the focus is on the archetypal and spiritual content, rather than the dream's personal associations. If a dream suggests a purely personal meaning it is rarely interpreted; usually the dreamer is advised to explore its associations for him or herself. This Sufi dreamwork does not intend to provide a substitute for in-depth analytic work, but rather to point out the spiritual and/or psychological context within which dreamers can realise for themselves, and in their own time, the full implications of their dreams. Similarly, the discussion and interpretation of the dream is not intended as a complete explanation of its meaning. It is a means of exploring the spiritual and psychological processes encountered on this Sufi Path. Often the full interpretation is only hinted at. And sometimes the dream is not

interpreted, but left to speak its own symbolic message to
those who can understand. Such is the way this dreamwork
has been practised for centuries, and so it continues to be
practised today.

This Sufi group belongs to the Naqshbandiyya-
Mujaddidiyya Dynasty, the Indian branch of Naqshbandi
Sufi Order. *Daughter of Fire: a Diary of a Spiritual Training
with a Sufi Master,* by Irina Tweedie, offers the most complete exposition of the Naqshbandiyya-Mujaddidiyya System,
and therefore I will refer to it in some detail. In fact, in
Daughter of Fire Irina Tweedie records a dream that suggests
that the book she would write about her spiritual training
would describe this Sufi System:

> I remember that I was telling other people, pointing to a thick
> book: 'In this book here is everything about his [my Teacher's]
> System. He gave it to me, I need not worry!' I knew in my
> dream that he gave me the book; it was mine and I need not be
> concerned about knowledge. But how he gave it to me is not
> clear. Only the book was clear; it was a thick volume bound in
> hardboard cover bound with heavy lines of yellow and it seemed
> blue. And it was new, which is surprising, really, a book on his
> System would be an old one, would it not? And I was pleased
> in my dream about the book which was mine.[3]

The cover of the 'book' in this dream has 'heavy lines of
yellow', which refers to the colour of this Sufi Line, which
is golden yellow. Blue, however, is the colour of devotion,
and is often associated with the feminine; it is the colour of
the Great Mother, and 'of the Virgin Mary as Queen of
Heaven'.[4] Therefore, the fact that this book 'seemed blue'
reflects the devotional nature of this Path; it is a feminine
Way to God. Before exploring in any depth the individual
dreams of members of the group I shall give a brief outline
of this particular Sufi System, and its traditional approach to
dreams.

THE NAQSHBANDI PATH

Sufism itself is a much more advanced psychological
system than all the systems developed so far in the
occidental world. This psychology in its essence is not
Eastern but Human (Idries Shah).

Sufism is a mystical Path of love, in which Truth, or God,
is found within the heart. Although it is often identified with
Islam, Sufism is older, older than any of the major religions.
It is neither a religion, nor a philosophy, but a way of life:

Sufism always was; it is the ancient wisdom. Only before the
Prophet they were not called Sufis. Long before they were a sect
called 'Kamal Posh' (blanket wearers), and they went to every
prophet. A tradition goes that they even went to Jesus. No one
could satisfy them. Every Prophet told them, do this or that,
and they were not satisfied. One day Mohammed said: 'There
are many Kamal Posh men coming, and they will reach here in
so many days and now at that moment they are there and there.'
They came when he said and on the day he said. And when they
were with him, he only looked at them without speaking. They
were completely satisfied.[1]

Why were they completely satisfied? Because he created love
in their hearts. 'When love is created what dissatisfaction can
there be?'

Thus the 'Kamal Posh' became assimilated into Islam; and
then, a century after the death of Mohammed, small circles
began to emerge throughout the Muslim world who were
known as 'Travellers' or 'Wayfarers on the Mystical Path'
reflecting a saying ascribed to the Prophet:

Be in this world as if you are a traveller, a passer-by, with your
clothes and shoes full of dust. Sometimes you sit under the shade

of a tree, sometimes you walk in the desert. Be always a passer-
by, for this is not home.

Due to their deep passion and longing, these mystics
realised the Truth as 'The Beloved', and were therefore also
known as 'The Lovers of God'. They became known as Sufis
only a few centuries after the death of the Prophet. Possibly,
this was a reference to the white woollen garment (*Suf*)
which allegedly they wore in common with the ancient
prophets and ascetics, or possibly it was an indication of the
purity of heart (*Safa*), which was the prerequisite for their
spiritual search. 'Sufi' could also be a derivation of the Greek
word *Sophia* (wisdom).

These small groups and circles, who gathered round a
spiritual Teacher, matured in time into fraternities and
orders. These were called Paths (*tarīqa*). The essence of the
Path is the tradition which links the succession of Teachers
in an uninterrupted chain of transmission. The image of the
Path is that of a spoke – one of innumerable spokes of a
wheel, leading from the outer circumference (= earthly life
governed by religious law) into the hub (= the Ultimate
Truth, the Heart of Hearts, the Beloved). Since the twelfth
century, these fraternities and Paths have crystallised into
well-defined orders, each one of them bearing the name of
its initiator. One of the most powerful, spiritually, has been
the Naqshbandiyya, named after Bahā ad-dīn Naqshband
(d. 1390). This Path has also been known as the Path of the
Masters. This is because it is descended from Khwāja Yūsuf
al-Hāmadāni, the first of the Khwājagān, or Masters of
Wisdom. The Masters of Wisdom were a powerful lineage
of Sufi Shaikhs who had a great influence on the spiritual life
of Asia Minor in the twelfth and thirteenth centuries. The
Naqshbandi Dynasty can be traced back through Yūsuf al-
Hāmadāni and a number of other Masters, including Abū
Yazīd al-Bīstāmī,[2] to the father-in-law of the Prophet, who
was the first Deputy.

Since its emergence, the Teachers of the Naqshbandi Path
concentrated their teachings on a number of principles. First
and foremost is the silent Recollection of God (*dhikr khafii*).
This is the recollection of the heart which is practised in every

thought, in every step, in each and every breath. While other Paths practised their *dhikr* with music, sacred songs and dancing, Bahā ah-dīn Naqshband stressed that the *dhikr* should be practised in silence. God is the silent Emptiness and, therefore, He is most easily reached in silence.

Another principle is 'Solitude in the Crowd': rather than shunning earthly duties, choosing an ascetic or monastic path, the Naqshbandi Teachers teach their disciples to be involved in life without being attached to its values. Thus these Wayfarers are encouraged to live an 'ordinary' life, to marry, bring up a family, have a profession and work in the world. Naqshbandis were often craftsmen, shoemakers, tailors, weavers (Bahā ad-dīn Naqshband was supposed to have been a potter), and this tradition still continues today, with many Wayfarers being artists or craftsmen, as well as others following different professions. And because they never wear any distinctive dress, Naqshbandis are able to work within the community without attracting undue attention, without creating a barrier between themselves and other people. Because the Naqshbandi Masters 'work entirely within the social framework of the culture in which they operate, in the Middle East and Central Asia [they] have gained the repute of being mainly Muslim pietists'.[3] In fact, there are Sufis working within Christian, Hindu and Buddhist as well as Muslim communities. Irina Tweedie's Teacher was a Hindu, while his Teacher was a Muslim.

But at the same time as being 'in the world' the Naqshbandi has to keep the fire of the internal journey kindled, as well as devotion to the Teacher, the Spiritual Guide. The focus of the Wayfarer is always towards the inner world of the heart and its longing for the Beloved, and thus he remains free from any identification with his outward activity. True poverty, in the Naqshbandi tradition, is non-attachment. This is the poverty of the Heart.

Within the apparently mundane existence of 'ordinary' life the Naqshbandi Teachers lead their followers through a subtle and extremely powerful path of inner experiences. The intensity of these experiences and the lack of any security forge into the psyche of the disciple the notions of Trust and Surrender. At the same time they also strengthen the sense and meaning of the 'Brotherhood'. While enduring the frequent confusion and psychological disturbance evoked both by external circumstances and inner states, one is not alone, but held and supported by one's fellow Wayfarers on the Path.

The Naqshbandi Path has a strong psychological orientation. Rather than being subjected to intense physical discomfort as in some other disciplines, the follower of this Path mainly experiences psychological pressure. It is for this reason that dreams and their interpretation have always been regarded as important.

The value that Sufis attach to dreams can be seen in the earliest Sufi manuals, which have sections on dreams. These often differentiate between 'true' and 'false' dreams; the latter being dreams without psychological or spiritual value. 'True dreams' are those which offer guidance, and one text describes how the 'reality' of such a dream is 'in the ideas revealed to the heart in those states which only descend upon our hearts when sleep has completely overwhelmed our consciousness'.[4] For the Sufi, 'reality' always belongs to the heart.

One ninth-century Sufi whose copious writings have a definite psychological orientation is al-Ḥakīm al-Tirmidhī. Although al-Tirmidhī lived over four centuries before Bahā ad-dīn Naqshband, he belongs to the same spiritual tradition, and was indeed a direct influence on Bahā ad-dīn, as the latter acknowledges in the following statement. The importance of al-Tirmidhī's influence is reflected in this statement's allusion to a mystical state that lies at the core of the Sufi Path, the fact that the Sufi becomes so absorbed in the formless Reality, that he becomes 'featureless':

> Twenty-two years I have been following in the footsteps of al-Tirmidhī. He had no feature and now I have no feature. Those who know will know and those who understand will understand.[5]

In an autobiographical sketch al-Tirmidhī recorded many of the dreams which helped guide him.[6] In one he saw an old man wearing white clothes and shoes, who said to him 'The prince tells you to be just.' As with this dream, he declares

that many are too obvious to need interpretation. Interestingly, he also describes dreams that his wife had for him,
where she played the part of a 'messenger'. In one such
dream she was shown a dry tree with withered branches,
springing out of a rocky barren land. A bird appeared and,
alighting on the tree, commenced to hop from branch to
branch. Wherever the bird touched the tree green leaves and
bunches of grapes appeared. However, she was given the
message that the tree must be looked after, otherwise the bird
would not be able to go to the topmost branches, but only
halfway up the tree. Grapes are a powerful Sufi symbol
representing esoteric teaching; moreover, from the grape is
made the wine of the Beloved that intoxicates the Sufi:

> Such a wine your love-lorn glance
> Served up to lovers, that knowledge
> Became unknowing and reason senseless.[7]

Thus the dream tells al-Tirmidhī to look after the tree of his
life and teachings, so that the bird of divine inspiration could
fully transform it, and produce grapes to nourish those who
lived in a spiritually barren land.

The twelfth-century Sufi, Najm ad-dīn Kubrā (1145–
1220), who was a pupil of Yūsuf al-Hamadānī, stressed the
importance of dreams and their interpretation, including in
the rules of the Path, along with 'constant silence, constant
retreat and constant recollection of God', 'constant direction
of a shaikh who explains the meanings of one's dreams and
visions.'[8] And Bahā ad-dīn Naqshband himself was
renowned as an interpreter of dreams.

DAUGHTER OF FIRE

In this century, in *Daughter of Fire*, Irina Tweedie gives a
contemporary autobiographical account of a spiritual training with a Naqshbandi Sufi Master. He regarded her dreams
as offering important guidance. He ordered her to keep a
diary:

> I would like you to keep a dairy, day-by-day entries of all your

experiences. And also keep a record of your dreams. Your dreams you must tell me, and I will interpret them for you. Dreams are important; they are a guidance.[9]

Daughter of Fire records many of Irina Tweedie's dreams, some of which are interpreted, as, for example, the following dream which images the slow process of becoming nothing before God:

> DREAM: I was looking at myself in a mirror and saw that I was very thin, very pale, my hair in disorder.
> INTERPRETATION: It is a very good dream! Thin and thinner until nothing will remain.[10]

But other dreams are not interpreted, sometimes because it was not appropriate to give the meaning at that time, and sometimes, as with al-Tirmidhī, because their meaning is quite clear, as when Irina Tweedie dreamt that she was in a hospital and her heart was being examined by a doctor with a stethoscope. To this dream her Teacher responded: 'Interpretation is not needed. The symbology is quite clear: your heart is being examined.'[11]

The Sufi Master in *Daughter of Fire* belongs to the Naqshbandi-Mujaddidi Dynasty, which, as I have mentioned, is the Indian branch of the Naqshbandiyya (named after Shaikh Ahmad Sirhindi, the Mujaddid (Renewer) (1564–1634)). Although Irina Tweedie's Teacher had no knowledge of contemporary psychology, she discovered that his method of training had definite psychological qualities:

> I became more and more fascinated by the discovery that the training devised by the tradition of Yoga thousands of years ago is absolutely identical with certain modern psychological criteria of today.[12]

One aspect of the psychological orientation of this training was the significance the Teacher attached to dreams and their interpretation; indeed it was because of one of Irina Tweedie's dreams that he sent her back from India to England in the middle of her training.[13] However, he said that before a dream can be interpreted it is necessary to know 'from where the dream comes'; for there are many different types of dreams. Similarly, in the dreamwork practised within our group, it is important to be able to identify the 'type of dream', because a psychological approach is not always appropriate. Some dreams are just 'mind dreams' in which the mind works over previous happenings or impressions. Yet sometimes dreams which apparently are just 'mind dreams' have a spiritual purpose in that when one is committed to the Path, karmas can go away in dreams:

> When you are on the Path earnestly and seriously, your Karmas are taken away from you. Either you have to suffer them . . . in your physical life, or they will come to you in dream. One second of dream-suffering is like three years of real suffering in life. When you are on the Path you are speeded up, and you pay for them in your dreams. If you stay away from the Path, once decided, all the Karmas you will pay in full in your daily life. But once on the Path, the Grace of God reaches you, catches up with you, and the mental Karmas will go away in dreams.[14]

Physical karmas must be suffered in the physical body, emotional karmas are burnt up by the tremendous longing for God, but 99½ per cent of the karmas 'are dealt with in dreams'.

Some dreams are 'past-life dreams', describing happenings from previous incarnations; and as such cannot be psychologically interpreted. Other dreams have a prophetic quality, pointing to future psychological, spiritual or even physical happenings. Irina Tweedie records a 'future' dream that points to the process of 'merging with the Teacher', *Fanā fi'l-Shaikh*, which is a very important part of the Sufi Path:[15]

> DREAM: I was dressed in black as for a lecture. I looked in the mirror and saw that I had a beard . . . a white beard around my face, as Muslims have. No other hair was on my cheeks, only the beard about three inches long, like a white, soft halo around the lower part of my face. Strange, that I go on lecturing to large audiences all over the world and nobody laughed at me, nobody called me a woman with a beard. Nobody seems to notice it . . .[16]

Many years later, when Irina Tweedie was in fact lecturing

to 'large audiences all over the world', people in the audience would occasionally 'see' her as having a beard.

When people first come to the group they often have dreams that indicate future psychological and spiritual developments (see Chapter 3). Such dreams can cffer encouragement and direction to the student, as when a dreamer saw that her eyes had changed and become golden green, 'deep pools of stillness and peace'.[17] But some prophetic dreams are 'warning dreams', for example, the following dream indicates that there will be a lot of emotional disturbance, relating to the therapy which the dreamer is having, but her family will not be disturbed, indeed they will not even notice:

> There is a flood which covcrs the land. I am very worried, but members of my family do not appear to take any notice, they still go about their daily business, i.e. my uncle goes to post a letter.

The figures in a person's dream generally image aspects of his own psyche, and part of working with a dream is understanding what the different figures in a dream mean. For example, why did the unconscious choose to portray a childhood friend or a distant relative? The dreamer's associations with the particular figure are usually the clue. Often it is the feeling associated with the dream figure that points to its symbolic meaning; a particular person evokes a certain feeling, and it is this aspect of oneself that the dream is imaging. And if one dreams of the Teacher, it usually refers to the inner teacher, the wise old man or wise old woman who is a personification of the Higher Self.

However, sometimes people have dreams which are for others, as with those of the wife of al-Tirmidhī. This happens also within our Sufi group, and the following dream gave a clear message to the individual concerned that he was now prepared to make the ultimate sacrifice that spiritual life demands. A friend had a dream in which this individual was arranging a red and white rose together, and then the Teacher said 'Now you are interested in spiritual life.' The symbolism of the dream relates to the custom of never giving an arrangement of red and white flowers to a hospital patient, because this combination is associated with death. Spiritual life demands the 'death' of the ego.

On some occasions dreams give spiritual teachings (see Chapter 7), as in the following two dreams, the first from the ninth century, the second from the twentieth century. The ninth-century Sufi, Abū Yazīd al-Bistāmī, had a dream, and in this dream he asked God 'What is the way to reach You?' He received the simple answer, 'The renunciation of self. Renounce the self and just walk in a straight way.' Recently, a friend was in a state of confusion – nothing in his life seemed to really make sense. Then he had a dream in which he was in a house that represented his confusion. He walked out of the house and met a man and a woman. He knew that the woman was going to tell him a truth, and at first he resisted hearing what she had to say. But then she spoke to him and said: 'Your confusion is because you have strayed from the house of God.' For a ninth-century Sufi saint and a twentieth-century man, a dream helped each on his Way to God.

In his autobiographical sketch, Al-Tirmidhī also records a 'teaching dream' in which he was shown a chair in the desert and told, 'This will lead you to God.' In this way he was told that his Path to God was in being a spiritual Teacher. Both this dream and the dream of Abū Yazīd would appear to be experiences on another plane of consciousness rather than actual dreams. For when the body is asleep, the soul is free: 'the king is not in his castle, the prisoner is not in his cell' and there are other planes of existence besides the physical. Moreover, when Irina Tweedie told her Teacher of a dream in which she met one of the Superiors of this line of Sufis, he said 'Many Great Beings come in the dreams; there are many Superiors on our Line.'[18]

Dreams which are 'experiences' have a particular quality which is most easily recognisable when they are told by the dreamer. Such dreams cannot be interpreted psychologically, but they are an attempt by the mind to convey as fully as possible an experience on a plane of consciousness which is totally different to that of our everyday world. The dreams of Abū Yazīd and al-Tirmidhī are able to be understood by the mind. The same is true of a dream in which the Teacher asked the dreamer, 'Have you ever had the experience/ turmoil of loving everybody all of the time?' But on other occasions, they point to a level of reality totally beyond our mental comprehension. One friend described a dream in which the Teacher talked about having made a journey to the very heart of the spiritual world which was experienced as music, and when the Teacher came back there were spare notes like bars of light stuck in her clothes and shoes, just as you might find sand in your shoes after being on the beach.

However, many dreams are primarily psychological, and symbolically describe the processes of inner transformation. The use of modern psychology and its approach to dreams helps the Wayfarer to benefit from these dreams and the guidance which they offer. Throughout the ages, Sufism has always remained alive and 'preserved its dynamism' through adapting and changing with the times, and yet at the same time remaining true to the essence of the tradition. Psychology provides a contemporary language with which the Wayfarer can more fully understand the eternal drama of the soul, a drama which is enacted within everyone who is committed to walking the lonely road towards the Truth.

A JUNGIAN APPROACH
TO SUFI DREAMWORK

> When you see a Sufi studying or teaching something
> that seems to belong to a field other than spirituality
> you should know that *there* is the spirituality of the age
> (Zahid).

The dreamwork within this Sufi group has a strong Jungian
orientation. This reflects the similarities between the spiritual
training in the Naqshbandi System and the Jungian
process of individuation. The practice of the silent meditation
of the heart has the effect of energising the psyche so that its
contents are brought into consciousness. In particular, the
individual is brought face to face with the darkness within,
with the 'shadow'. As Irina Tweedie comments:

Perfection brings imperfection to the surface

> I had hoped to get instructions in Yoga, expected wonderful
> teachings, but what the Teacher did was mainly to force me to
> face the darkness within myself, and it almost killed me. In other
> words he made me 'descend into hell,' the cosmic drama enacted
> in every soul as soon as it dares lift its face to the Light.[1]

For Irina Tweedie, it was the yogic powers of her Teacher
which evoked her inner darkness in a dramatic and often
terrifying manner. She was on the Road of *Tyaga*, or
complete Renunciation, while most who follow this Sufi
System are on the Road of *Dhyana*. This is the slower Road,
on which the unconscious, activated through silent meditation, is experienced more gradually. None the less, the
individual follows the same path, first into the world of the
personal shadow, and then into deeper archetypal realms.
Everyone experiences the unconscious in dreams and in

states of inner turbulence. But a psychological phenomenon of this Path is that ordinary, everyday situations become more highly charged, as the activated contents of the unconscious seek expression. Thus, situations that from a 'normal' perspective might seem trivial or unimportant can become highly dynamic psychologically. In particular, the group dynamics within this Sufi group can be very powerful. It is as if ordinary, everyday situations and relationships become a stage on which the inner *opus* is highly dramatised; what the alchemists saw projected into their retorts and crucibles, the Sufis see projected on to their worldly environment. The process of individuation is thus 'speeded up' as day-to-day living becomes psychologically intensified.

Jung

For the Sufi, experiencing the pressure of inner and outer situations, Jung's work is very important in that, within the field of modern psychology, he has most fully charted this inner mythic quest that has the Reality of the Self as its goal. His study of the psychological manifestations of the Self, its symbols and dynamics, is the most complete within this field. And in what Jung regarded as his final important work, *Mysterium Coniunctionis*, he gives a comprehensive description of the different psychological stages in the 'individual's discovery of the self'. Moreover, Jung speaks with the authority of experience, for he has *been there*. He is not merely describing psychological concepts, but an inner imaginal land which he explored as fully as possible. In *Memories, Dreams, Reflections* Jung states that it was his own descent into the unconscious, which lasted for a period of four years, that formed the basis, the *prima materia*, for his lifetime's work:

> This was the primal stuff which compelled me to work upon it, and my works are a more or less successful endeavour to incorporate this incandescent matter into the contemporary picture of the world.[2]

Jung's own experience of the unconscious had a profoundly spiritual quality, and his work reflects the awe of one who has touched and been touched by the divine within himself. The numinous nature of the inner world underlies his attempt to portray the dynamics of the psyche scientifically. This is of the utmost importance for the seeker who is trying to combine the spiritual and the psychological in his or her own inner work.

Jungian psychology thus offers an invaluable means for the Western mind to understand, as far as possible, the psychological processes encountered on the Path. For example, in Sufi texts there is a prolific occurrence of pairs of opposites, (e.g. 'qurb' (nearness) and 'bu'd' (separation)) which 'refer to psychological states or stages of the Sufi on his way to spiritual realization'.[3] Thus the Sufi is thrown, often violently, between these opposites, a phenomenon which has been termed in our group the 'Yo-Yo Syndrome'. This process, which is experienced by everyone on the Path, is a continual fluctuation between up and down: one day you feel wonderful and meditation goes very well, then the next day you feel awful, and feel that you are not progressing at all, and meditation seems hopeless. In *Mysterium Coniunctionis* Jung offers a psychological explanation for this phenomenon, describing it as the reconciliation of opposites:

> Ascent and descent, above and below, up and down, represent an emotional realization of opposites, and this realization gradually leads, or should lead, to their equilibrium. This motif occurs very frequently in dreams, in the form of going up- and downhill, climbing stairs, going up or down in a lift, balloon, aeroplane etc . . . As Dorn interprets it, this vacillating between the opposites and being tossed back and forth means being contained *in* the opposites. They become a vessel in which what was previously now one thing and now another floats vibrating, so that the painful suspension between opposites gradually changes into a bilateral activity of the point in the centre. This is the 'liberation from opposites,' the *nirdvandva* of Hindu philosophy, though it is not really a philosophical development.'[4]

The experience of the opposites has great psychological significance, for it can be associated with the development of consciousness. In the original state of undifferentiated wholeness everything is experienced as a part of the whole, in what Levy-Bruhl describes as a state of *participation mystique*.[5] This uroboric state can be seen in the early life of a child. Initially, it lives in complete oneness with the Self, which Neumann

[margin note: The Yo-Yo Syndrome]

calls the original uroboric state.[6] Ideally, this oneness is experienced externally, in a feeling of oneness with life and the mother. But slowly, the world of duality dawns with the coming of consciousness. For the child, the first experience of the opposites is often the 'good breast' and the 'bad breast', for it is a common experience that one breast feeds more easily than the other. But as the ego of the child develops there is a separation from Self, often experienced as a separation between the individual self and the outside world, or between child and mother. Thus the baby leaves the paradise of oneness for the duality of the world of the ego. Only on the level of the Self can this original oneness again be experienced.

At the birth of the consciousness of mankind stands the experience of the opposites, and the first pair of opposites to appear in the dawn of humanity must have been the primal division between life and death. Everything in this world is caught between the tension of these great opposites, and they stand at the gateway to consciousness. It is man's awareness of life and death that pushes him to go beyond their limitations. Prince Hamlet mused 'To be or not to be, that is the question:' but later he became aware of a greater pattern that lies behind these opposites:

> There's a divinity that shapes our ends,
> Rough-hew them how we will.[7]

All spiritual paths, all religious systems are born from this tension between life and death. And they point to a 'liberation' from these opposites to the world of the soul, or the Self, that contains the opposites and yet lies beyond them.

The birth of individual consciousness is reflected in an experience of the opposites; and this experience becomes emphasised in the process of 'individuation', Jung's term for the individual's journey towards psychological wholeness.[8] The moment the individual begins to work on himself there appears the primal division between consciousness and the unconscious, between the ego and the shadow, between what you think you are, and what you discover you are. As the seeker starts to acknowledge his own faults and inadequacies, so he is confronted with his own darkness.

What had been projected on to the outside world needs to be owned as belonging to himself.

> The individual's specious unity that emphatically says '*I* want, *I* think' breaks down under the impact of the unconscious. So long as [the individual] can think that somebody else (his father or mother) is responsible for his difficulties, he can save some semblance of unity . . . But once he realizes that he himself has a shadow, that his enemy is in his own heart, then the conflict begins and one becomes two.[9]

An awareness of the opposites in one's own nature at first brings conflict, and the individual is thrown, often violently, between the two. This is a very painful process, for one loses any stable identity, and instead, experiences an inner battle, as opposing aspects of oneself fight it out. On this battlefield previously unacknowledged parts of oneself demand to be recognised, demand 'a place in the sun'. The importance of this conflict, together with its painful nature, is expressed in Christ's seemingly paradoxical statement:

> Think not that I am come to send peace on earth: I came not to send peace, but a sword.
> For I am to set man at variance against his father, and the daughter against her mother, and the daughter-in-law against her mother-in-law.[10]

Christ is a symbol of psychological wholeness: he embraced both Mary the Virgin, and Mary Magdalene, the whore. But, in order to realise one's wholeness, it is first necessary to encounter the opposites, a process referred to in the alchemical *opus* as the *separatio*. In Christian symbolism this state is imaged by the crucifixion:

> whoever finds himself on the path of individuation cannot evade that suspension between the opposites which is symbolized by the crucifixion.[11]

On the path of individuation, not only is there the duality of the ego and shadow, but also the awareness of the contra-sexual aspect of the psyche, the animus and anima. And, for the seeker after Ultimate Truth, there is the most important duality, that of ego and Self; the sense of individual identity and the Reality in which there is no 'I', only Oneness. As in Abū Yazīd's dream, quoted earlier, the renunciation of the ego (self with a small 's') is considered by the Sufi as the basis of the spiritual path. The best way to reach Him is 'To renounce the self and just walk in a straight way'. The ego belongs to the world of duality, and if one is to experience His Unity, one must transcend the ego. The ego must be continually sacrificed, the Wayfarer follow His will, and not the desires of the ego. Here the psychological and spiritual directions are different, for psychological individuation aims towards an integrated, balanced ego, while the Sufi seeks for a world beyond the ego.

But before the ego can be transcended, the individual must experience the tension between the opposites; he or she must experience the full intensity of this world of duality. The spiritual path is not an escape from this world, but a highly dynamic journey through it. And as Jung suggests, it is through being 'tossed back and forth', through experiencing this conflict, that one reaches the 'liberation from opposites', the still centre of the pendulum. It is here, between the opposites, that the spiritual world has the most direct influence on the individual:

> Why is it important to get somewhere into the centre of the pendulum. Because here between the opposites lie all the possibilities of growth. Here influences from a higher level can reach us! Here in this place where one can feel one's nothingness and be free from contradictions.[12]

This is the purpose of the Zen koan. The student meditates upon a paradoxical statement which usually contains a pair of irreconcilable opposites. For example:

> When you meet a Zen master on the road you cannot talk to him, you cannot face him with silence. What are you going to do?[13]

Thrown between the opposites, the mind of the student eventually surrenders, and he or she is then open to the spiritual realm where Truth is a paradox. For the Sufi, the conflicting opposites are usually experienced psychologically, but the dynamic is the same. When the tension between the poles becomes unbearable, the seeker can only surrender himself to the Beloved, to That within himself that both contains and transcends the opposites. On the spiritual path the conflict of the opposites is used as a process of forcing the seeker beyond the world of duality. The opposites can be imagined as two ends of a piece of string: by pulling the centre of the string away at right angles the two opposing ends come together, the two become one.

Jungian psychology offers many invaluable insights into the psychological dynamics of the Sufi Path. However, it is also necessary to acknowledge its limitations. This is suggested by the following dream, which both embraces the idea of the reconciliation of opposites and looks beyond any psychological context:

> I am standing beside the Teacher, and behind me the group is on a fairground carousel, which is going round and round and up and down. Then a man comes and from a chest of drawers he takes out an orange robe, which is for me. I am a bit overawed by this robe, wondering whether it is really for me, but he gives it to me and tells me that I must finish the hem.

The image of the group on a carousel, going up and down and round and round, perfectly symbolises the dynamic of being thrown between the opposites on a Road that is not linear, but a circular journey towards wholeness. However, the image of the orange robe and the symbolic meaning of the dreamer finishing the hem cannot be appreciated from a solely psychological context. For the orange robe is associated with the *sannyasin*, one who has renounced the world, and thus finishing the hem of this robe suggests the completion of a certain spiritual work. And the hem of this robe echoes the hem of another garment:

> If you are able to touch, however gently,
> The hem of the garment of Truth,
> You have no other desire for the rest of your life,
> But to tell others who they are.[14]

The dream images the psychological processes of the Path, and at the same time it tells the dreamer that it is time to acknowledge the spiritual direction of her life. The robe, kept

in a chest of drawers, symbolises a spiritual commitment that
until now had not become conscious; and yet the dream
suggests that this robe had always belonged to the dreamer.
Within our unconscious our destiny is stored, and at the right
time in our life different aspects of this destiny become
manifest. Sometimes one can glimpse the deeper pattern of
one's life unfolding, and often, looking back, see how things
happened in the 'ripeness of time'. Some will meet their
Teacher when they are 20, while Irina Tweedie waited till
she was 56 to meet her Sufi Master. She recently surprised a
young man who was interviewing her, because, rather than
talking about 'spiritual matters', she told him of her life
before the war: how she used to eat in a different restaurant
each night and then dance until the early hours. Then she said
to the young man; 'And you, you should go and live fully.
Work hard, make love to your wife, enjoy drinking beer and
bringing up your children. Then one day you will suddenly
wake up, and say "There must be more to life." And then
spiritual life will begin for you.' And the man agreed. He
said that he felt he had a lot to do in the world before starting
on a spiritual quest.

The realisation of a spiritual 'call' happens not through the
will of the ego, but the prompting of the soul. For our
dreamer the orange robe told her that it was now time to
turn away from the world, towards Home, and the fact that
she was 'overawed' reflects a deep understanding of the
nature of this journey.

Both Jungian psychology and the Sufi Path point the
human being towards the Self. And yet the individuation
process does not have a primarily spiritual orientation. It is
only because the spiritual dimension is that most lacking in
our materialistic society that the psychological path towards
wholeness needs to orientate the individual in that direction:

> The individuation process is directed first and foremost to the
> completeness of the personality. Its constant aim is to raise out
> of the unconscious the 'missing' element that would make for
> wholeness, and to join it to consciousness. In our materialisti-
> cally oriented world, therefore, the prime task will be spirituali-
> zation, the *opus contra naturam*.[15]

Moreover, while the psychological goal of individuation offers the visible aim of resolving conflicts and living a more balanced life, the Sufi is interested only in a pathless path towards an invisible goal. Thus the seeker is imaged as an arrow, aimed by an archer in the darkness at an invisible target; and the archer is the Beloved, who, burning in the heart of the seeker, fires him into the Void. Therefore, although psychological wholeness is undoubtably achieved on the spiritual path, it is not the aim. The Wayfarer's journey is to the Infinite. Indeed, Jacobi suggests that the individuation process is a *preparation* for the mystical encounter with God:

> The experience of God in the form of an encounter or '*unio mystica*' is the only possible and authentic way to a genuine belief in God for modern man. The individuation process can 'prepare' a man for such an experience. It can open him to the influence of a world beyond his rational consciousness, and give him insight into it . . . One might say that in the course of the individuation process a man arrives at the entrance to the house of God.[16]

Thus, the process of individuation and the psychological work it involves, whether alone or with the help of an analyst, is seen as a necessary preliminary stage on the Path.

> We must live within the very turmoil of life, but not be influenced by it. We must get rid of likes and dislikes. We must return to the very core of our primitive being in order to become whole. This will naturally produce conflicts, for we have to accept ourselves as we are and not as we THINK WE ARE.[17]

In practice seekers are confronted by psychological situations that force them into the depths; and in accepting what they find there they ground themselves in the depths of their being, and so have a firm foundation for spiritual life. This process is illustrated by a dream of a man who had a particularly difficult relationship with his father, a relationship that demanded intense psychological work. When this relationship was nearly resolved, the man had the following dream:

> I went with my father to the bottom of a spiral, stone staircase.

Then, leaving my father at the foot of the stairs, I climbed up on my own. When I reached the top I was met by Guru Maharaj, the Guru of my Guru, and invited to a *satsang* [sitting in the presence of the Teacher] with him. He gave me some symbolic articles of jewellery, and then showed a film of himself as a young man flying a kite.

This dream suggests that the dreamer's difficult relationship with his father, and the self-discovery that this involved, took him to a point where, proceeding alone, he was able to climb to a higher 'level', and there receive the spiritual teachings imaged by the *satsang*, the jewellery and the film. This last image of the young man flying the kite teaches that in spiritual life one can only 'fly high' if one's feet are firmly on the ground.

The teaching of the young man and the kite points to the place where the psychological and the spiritual paths finally divide. For psychology focuses on our life here, in this world, 'on the ground'. It aims to understand the dynamics of the psyche and the Self in relation to individual consciousness. Thus Jung continually orientated his work away from the vagaries of mysticism towards *this* world:

I aimed, after all, at *this* world, and *this* life. No matter how deeply absorbed or how blown about I was, I always knew that everything I was experiencing was ultimately directed at this real life of mine.[18]

And although he was convinced of the importance of the Self, Jung appeared to reject any conscious experience beyond the limited perception of the ego:

We can only *say* that the self is limitless, but we cannot *experience* its infinity.[19]

The Sufi experiences this world in all its beauty, in all its richness, and is acutely sensitive to its suffering; and yet, at the same time he regards it as Maya, or an illusion:

Those who are always with their Guru do not possess worldly things.
  They rest in their Guru, and everything else does not touch them.[20]

And the disciple's only reality is the limitless world of the Self. Thus the Sufi aims to transcend individual consciousness in a mystical union with the Beloved; and here Jung's own description of the *unio mystica* in itself suggests the limitations of a psychological perspective:

> that absolute reality where one is nothing but psychic reality, yet confronted with the psychic reality that one is not . . . The ego disappears completely. The psychical is no longer a content in us, but we become contents of it . . . this condition . . . is almost unimaginable.[21]

For the Wayfarer, there comes a moment when a psychological approach is no longer appropriate, as is beautifully imaged in the following dream:

> I am driving up a hill in my old Volvo. The hill gets steeper and steeper, and so I change gears, from first to second, then second to third and finally third to fourth. But the hill is still too steep for me to drive up. Just as I am waking from the dream I realize that it would be much easier just to get out and walk.

The dreamer was a man who had had a number of years of Jungian analysis, and was very influenced by Jungian ideas. When discussing the dream, he understood the old car as representing the Jungian idea of wholeness and individuation, one of whose aims is to develop the use of all the four functions.[22] Normally when driving a car up a hill one would change *down*, from fourth to third to second etc., here the dreamer changed *up*, i.e. had to use more of his four functions. But even the fourth gear, suggestive of wholeness, was insufficient. How much simpler just to get out and walk! On the spiritual path *everything* must be left behind, even the idea of psychological integration. One goes to Him as naked as when one first came into the world.

For the Sufi, psychological work is fundamental but only preparatory. It is a process of working on the psyche, cleaning it out, emptying it of all the rubbish and chaos which has accumulated and also been inherited. We begin on the Path filled up and overflowing; not only full of our own psychological conflicts and problems, but also of those of our parents and other aspects of our conditioning. When we are in this state we cannot receive anything. A prospective disciple once came to a Zen Master and asked to become his pupil, to which the Zen Master answered by offering him a cup of tea. The young man held out his cup and the Master poured in the tea, but when the cup was full he continued pouring, and the tea spilled all over the man's clothes. Eventually, in great dismay, the man said to the Master, 'Look, can't you see the cup is full!' To which the Master replied, 'Yes, and so are you. You come here full to the brim and expect me to teach you something?'

Psychological work is a process of forging within the psyche of the disciple the empty cup that is then to be filled with the wine of the Beloved. Because finally, spiritual life is a question of grace, and the lover can only wait, longing to be embraced by his Beloved. And He comes when He wants, in His own time, and often at the least expected moment. Then your heart is suddenly filled with bliss; you are touched with love in the innermost part of your being. It is in this sense that the Sufi Master in *Daughter of Fire* called the Naqshbandi System 'effortless'; for although the seeker must work hard upon himself, descend into the very depths of the psyche, any mystical state remains a divine gift, one that takes him beyond this world into a Reality which cannot be explained:

> Only things which cannot be explained are lasting. What can be comprehended with the mind is not a high state. If you cannot express it, cannot put it into words, those are things not of the mind, and they will go on forever.[23]

Thus the Sufi Path both includes and looks beyond Jungian psychology, and this will be reflected in any Sufi dream-work.

DREAMS ON FIRST COMING TO THE GROUP

When it is possible to hear the beloved speak himself,
why listen to second-hand reports? (Jami)

THE SPIRITUAL QUEST

Dreams can offer both psychological and spiritual guidance,
and such guidance is often given from the moment an
individual first comes to our group. Jung observed that when
the unconscious notices that something is to be done about
it, it will respond with a dream or a series of dreams. Often
just before or after a person comes to our group, they will
have an important dream, one that may point out the
direction of their spiritual path and the psychological work
that needs to be done. The following dream suggests that the
dreamer is ready for spiritual life and the real effort that this
involves:

> I am in a second-hand bookshop and there I see a second-hand
> pack of tarot cards. I think of buying them, but then I think that
> they may be incomplete, so I don't.

Central to this dream is the repeated image of something
'second-hand': a 'bookshop', a 'pack of tarot cards'. But the
dreamer rejects the tarot cards, because they may be incom-
plete: he does not want second-hand spiritual life, such as is
found in books, because he is aware that it will be incom-
plete. The true seeker is not interested in the knowledge
gained from books, but in the experiences of the soul on the
inward Path to the Truth. Therefore the Sufi Master does not
'teach' anything, but gives the disciple experiences: 'I am

giving you experiences and you do with it what you like.'[1]
Only the 'Knowledge of the Soul' is the 'Real Knowledge',
and this is realised from within, and thus becomes an integral
part of the seeker.

> The knowledge of the Soul . . . comes to the physical mind and
> then it becomes the Real Knowledge, the integral part of you.
> If I would tell you, and you would have faith enough and believe
> me, then the faith and the knowledge would be two things, is
> it not so? But like this, nothing is told. You will realize it in
> yourself; it becomes part of you; there is no duality . . .[2]

While this dream of the tarot cards makes a simple
statement about the dreamer's need for first-hand spiritual
knowledge, the following dream, which a woman told when
she first came to the group, describes her path in a detailed
series of symbolic images:

> I am walking on a tightrope. A man with a long fork comes and
> tries to get me down, but I take the fork from him and use it as
> a balancing pole. Then a pair of hands takes my shoulders, and
> like a trapeze artist I swing round and round. Then I fly through
> the air and come to a green fountain, underwater. I am happy
> underwater, and don't need to breathe, it is as if I breathe
> through gills. Then I am a fish and there is the figure of Neptune
> with a three pronged fork. He spears me. I 'come to' in a field
> with pain in three chakras. I put leaves on the pain. A small man
> comes and puts a gold ring around my left foot. On the ring is
> written 'God helps those who help themselves'. Then I am a
> buffalo in a herd of buffaloes, and I suddenly feel a searing pain
> in my shoulder as I am being branded. I am in McDonalds,
> eating a hamburger, and the smell is the same as the herd of
> buffaloes. I can't eat the hamburger and vomit.

A full appreciation of this dream would require a chapter
to itself, but in our dreamwork we tend to focus on those
aspects that are most spiritually significant. The spiritual path
is often imaged as a tightrope or narrow bridge. A famous
Zen picture by Hakuin, *Blind Men Crossing a Bridge*,[3] shows
the Path as a narrow bridge over a chasm, over which three
blind men are slowly groping their way. The seeker must
walk 'on the razor's edge', always keeping an inner balance;
and an early Christian mystic, St Gregory of Nyssa (*c.* 331–

c.396), describes the Path of Love as 'a Bridge of Hair Across a Chasm of Fire'. In the above dream, while the dreamer is walking on a tightrope, the shadow, in the form of Satan, 'A man with a long fork', tries to upset her balance. Only too often does this happen on the Path, as the shadow pulls us down, and time and again we fall. But here the dreamer takes the fork and uses it as a 'balancing pole'. This is a profound statement on how the shadow can in fact help us, offering insight into our inner nature, and, indeed, allowing us to become 'more balanced'.

Lifted and swung round, the dreamer is in the hands of God. Flying through the air she goes underwater, and the fact that she is happy there and doesn't need to breathe shows how she is at home in the unconscious. As a fish, she becomes at one with her unconscious nature, when she is speared, not by Satan, but by Neptune, Lord of the Sea. Neptune could here symbolise the divine aspect of the animus,[4] especially as she 'comes to' on dry land. It is the animus who helps the woman leave the waters of her own unconscious self for the dry land of consciousness,[5] though any such process of conscious awareness can often be painful, as imaged by the 'pain in three chakras'. This pain is healed through relating again to the natural world, 'leaves'. The 'gold ring around my left foot' has a profound Sufi symbolism. Slaves often had rings placed around their ankles, and Sufis are the 'slaves of God' ('slaves of the One and servants of the many'). The ring is gold, symbolising the transformation inherent in this slavery, and it also suggests the image of a wedding ring, for the Sufi is married to the Beloved. The fact that the ring is around the left foot implies that this whole process takes place through the unconscious,[6] which is a part of the feminine mystery of the surrender to God.

The saying 'God helps those who help themselves' needs no interpretation, except to say that it echoes a Sufi saying, 'First tie up your camel and then trust in God.' But the branding of the buffalo is highly symbolic. The buffalo is similar to the 'ox' of the Zen 'Oxherding Pictures', which images the instinctual self which is also the divine nature of man. This is our primal wholeness, 'our face before we were born'. That the dreamer becomes a buffalo symbolises that she is at one with her whole divine, instinctual self, and it is as a buffalo, as her divine Nature, that she is branded by God. For there are those who are branded by God, they belong only to Him; and this is echoed in a saying attributed to Christ: 'I know my sheep and my sheep know me.' Such people often find human relationships difficult, for deep within they know that they belong to Another.

> There are human beings who cannot create deep and lasting relationships with other human beings, because it is as if they are destined for Something Else. It is as if He, the Infinite One, put a mark on the heart of this human being, as if He would say 'This human being belongs to Me.'[7]

For those who are so branded, however much they may try and often painfully struggle to 'fit in' in this world, they never can; in their hearts they know that they belong somewhere else. For such people this world only has meaning as a Path to Him; and significantly, when the dreamer has been branded, ordinary life, a hamburger in McDonalds, is very difficult to digest, it makes her sick. Yet the dream also shows how in fact this world, imaged as a hamburger which reflects the smell and meat of the buffalo, embodies God's instinctual Self:

> the same world which deceived us with its multiplicity and variety, with its unnourishing prescriptions, with its facts which offended us, is also a representation of the Self which we are seeking. God's body is 'out there' in the world for all to see.[8]

At first, when one has seen through the illusion of the world and glimpsed the Beyond, physical existence becomes distasteful. But later, all becomes one and there is no sense of duality between the Creator and His creation. This is imaged in the final Oxherding picture, when the old man, the sage, goes to the market: 'He is found in company with winebibbers and butchers, he and they are all converted into Buddhas.'[9]

While the above dream images the Sufi as a slave of God,

the following dream describes the spiritual path as freeing the dreamer from the chains of this world. It was dreamt by a man soon after he first came to our group:

> I am on an island full of people drinking, laughing etc., but I know that a great storm and tidal wave is coming, so I go to a hill in the middle of the island and climb a tree. The storm comes and all the people are killed, but I just hang on and survive. Then after the storm a pirate ship comes to the island and takes me off as a slave, though I ask not to be chained and the pirates agree. They take me to a port where there is a slave market; all the other slaves are chained but they are paper chains. The paper chains then catch fire, and burn, but no one is burnt.

This dream begins with the dreamer as part of the concourse of life, 'people drinking, laughing'. This is the world of material existence, and yet it is on an island, suggesting that for the dreamer it embodies a certain isolation: he is isolated from his real Self. But a storm and tidal wave is coming: embarking on the spiritual path will bring a storm, a great inner disturbance that will destroy all these people, and leave the dreamer all alone. How often is this experienced by those who begin the spiritual quest, when worldly values and pursuits become empty and friends drop away, leaving one feeling alone. The door of this world closes behind you, and yet the next door has not yet opened. Rescued by a pirate ship the dreamer becomes a slave, though not chained. This image of a slave could refer to the dreamer becoming a slave of God, but the idea of slavery and chains also suggests another meaning. While most people in the world think that they are free, one of the first things that the seeker discovers on the Path is the chains of desire and conditioning that imprison him, and indeed the Arabic word for a human being, *'abd*, also carries the meaning of slave. The image of humanity as being enchained is present in Plato's cave analogy, where man is depicted as a prisoner since childhood, fastened by his legs and neck so that he can only look straight ahead at a wall on which shadows played, shadows which he assumes are the 'real things'.[10] Moreover, before one can become truly free of this world of illusion, one must be aware that one is chained, and paradoxically,

only those who become slaves of God are really free, free
from the chains of the *nafs* or ego.

When the dreamer is taken to the slave market, he sees that
all the other slaves are chained 'but they are paper chains'.
For the Sufi, the chains of this world can be burnt away by
the desire for Truth, and this is what happens in this dream.
Significantly, when these chains burn, the slaves are not
burnt. The fire that burns but does not burn has great
spiritual significance, echoing the fire in the Burning Bush
of Moses. This is the purifying fire of God, that burns away
the dross, the chains of this world. Thus this dream describes the unfolding of the dreamer's spiritual path on which,
as a slave, he is freed from chains that are made only of
paper.

The image of the fire that burns but does not burn is
echoed in another dream; again the dreamer is a man:

> I am watching my own birth, I am both father and the child.
> When I look at the child there is a feeling of great peace about
> him. Then I notice that there are flames on the bed, although the
> bed is not being burnt. The mother is worried but the child is
> not. I go to get water for the flames, but they are not put out.

The child, symbol of the Self, is born from within, 'the reborn is his own begetter'; and the 'feeling of great peace
about him' points to the divine nature of this 'child'. Furthermore, according to Jung, the fact that the child is identical
with the father means in psychological language that 'a
central archetype, the God-image, has renewed itself ("been
reborn") and become "incarnate" in a way perceptible to
consciousness.'[11]

The twelfth-century Sufi, Sohravardi (d. 1191), refers to
his own 'Perfect Nature' as being simultaneously the Bearer
of the Child and the Child who is Born. 'Perfect Nature' is
analogous to the Self, and an Arabic Hermetic text describes
how it is both the 'root' of man's being, and also the 'branch
springing from him':

> Wise Socrates declared the Perfect Nature is called the sun of the
> philosopher, the original *root* of his being and at the same time
> the *branch* springing from him. Hermes was asked: 'How does
> one achieve knowledge of wisdom? How can one bring it down

to this world below?' 'Through Perfect Nature,' he answered. 'What is the root of wisdom?' 'Perfect Nature.' 'What is the key to wisdom?' 'Perfect Nature.' 'What then is Perfect Nature?' he was asked. 'It is the heavenly entity, the philosopher's Angel, conjoined with his star, which rules him and opens the door of wisdom for him, teaches him what is difficult, reveals to him what is right, in sleeping as in waking.'[12]

Thus Perfect Nature, or the Self, is the Inner Guide who unlocks the wisdom within us, and in so doing gives birth to Himself. Furthermore, this 'heavenly entity' guides us 'in sleeping and in waking': during the day it appears in the form of inspiration, intuition, conscience etc. When we are asleep it guides us through dreams.

In the dream of the man watching his own birth, the flames that do not burn once again point to a spiritual fire, echoing the tongues of flame of the Holy Ghost. And while the mother is worried by these flames, the child is not; for although the spiritual energy imaged by these flames can be psychologically disturbing, it is the very substance of our divine nature. The final image of the dreamer being unable to 'put out' the flames emphasises their spiritual nature, for:

'The fire that is not put out is a holy fire' (Shaw, *Saint Joan*) . . . The unquenchable fire . . . is a well known attribute of the Deity, not only in the Old Testament, but also as an *allegoria Christi* . . . the Saviour himself says: Whoever is near to me is near to the fire; whoever is far from me is far from the kingdom.[13]

This fire is the fire of longing, the unquenchable flame in the heart that purifies the seeker, and relentlessly drives him along the Way. It is the longing that always burns and burns, taking the Wayfarer Home into the arms of the Beloved.

This dream images the mystery that lies at the centre of every spiritual path, the birth into consciousness of the divine nature of the seeker. And although this dream was told by someone who had only been a few times to our group, he had already been practising meditation for a number of years. He described his form of meditation as 'self-observation' or 'witnessing', which is reflected in the dream imagery of 'watching my own birth'. 'Witnessing' suggests the Sufi

notion of the 'Witness in Heaven', *shāhid fi'l-samā*, which is
similar to the Inner Guide or 'Perfect Nature'. The Witness
in Heaven watches us, and it is also that within us that
contemplates upon God. Through the eyes of the Witness
God sees us, and through those same eyes we can see Him;
in the words of Meister Eckhart, 'The seeing through which
I know him is the same seeing through which he knows me.'
By the practice of 'witnessing' the dreamer identifies with his
'Heavenly Witness', and through knowing himself he will
come to know God, for 'He who knows *himself* knows *his
Lord.*'

Not all those who attend a Naqshbandi group need to
practise the silent meditation of the heart, for the Sufi is
open-minded, and aware that 'there are as many ways to God
as there are breaths of the children of men'. What was
important for this dreamer was that in being in the company
of other sincere seekers of Truth, he was able to share his
own spiritual quest. His unconscious responded with a
dream that showed the direction of this quest; and in telling
this dream within a spiritual environment, he could more
fully appreciate its auspicious meaning, and the encouragement it gave to him to continue along the Path.

THE DESCENT INTO THE UNCONSCIOUS

'The Kingdom of Heaven is within', and the spiritual quest
is an inward journey into the depths of the unconscious. This
is the mythic 'Night Sea Journey', and many dreams help
guide the seeker across the inner waters of the psyche. These
dreams offer a psychological as opposed to a purely spiritual
direction, and often indicate the psychological work that
needs to be done. In the following dream the dreamer is
shown that his first objective is an encounter with the
'shadow', the aspects of himself that are rejected and undervalued, and so hidden in darkness:

> I was exploring a wild landscape, walking with difficulty
> through swampy or boggy ground. Nearby there was a enclosed
> area, like a fairground. I had a ticket and went through the
> turnstile. I entered a large building. I had to find the deepest,

darkest spot, from whence all the trouble arose. There were many corridors and rooms in the building and several floors. I went into quite a lot of rooms. Some were empty, some contained bits and pieces of furniture, and in some I met women, a different one in each room, most of them rather small, a bit shadowy, in early middle age. I hurried on, passing them all, as they were not what I was looking for. Then, in the last room, a very large, naked, very white-skinned woman, middle-aged and seemingly a giant, came towards me. I went up to her and stood exactly facing her, and saw that she was not so large after all, but exactly the same size as me. She was awe-inspiring. It occurred to me that we somehow corresponded. I could have stayed with her and there was a slight erotic fascination, but I went on because I knew I had not yet found what I needed to find. Round the next bend of the corridor I met two sinister men, like KGB officials, coming *for* me. I knew they were people who like me had come to this place, and could never, ever leave it. They were lacking in some essential human attribute (love?) and they were going to remove this same attribute from me. I was very frightened. I had no alternative but to accompany them. They took me to a large room, something like a physics laboratory. Inside were other similar men. Seated behind a table was a rather nondescript individual with glasses, (whom I had met as a person, just once, that day). He was the incarnation of all evil. The other men began to close in on me. I was terrified, the fear was greater than anything I have ever experienced, and I began to shout out 'God, God, God!'. As I did so I became aware of the street a long way below and people walking about there, and very vaguely the contours of the whole building. This could have constituted a way out of this hopeless situation. However I was shouting out 'God' aloud and woke up my wife and daughter, who woke me up.

This dream begins in a wild, swampy landscape, suggestive of the unknown, watery world of the unconscious. In this landscape the dreamer comes to a fairground, to which he has a ticket. In the context of this dream I would understand a fairground with all its strange and fantastical associations to describe an inner space where the figures of the imaginal can be encountered. It echoes the 'Magic Theatre' of Herman Hesse's *Steppenwolf*, a 'theatre' in which, behind different doors, is enacted various aspects of the unconscious of the protagonist, Harry Haller. And just as in

Hesse's 'Magic Theatre' entrance is 'Not For Everyone', so our dreamer must have a ticket to go in. The world of the unconscious cannot be entered without paying the price, for the experience of this 'fairground' means leaving the rational world and the values of the persona. In *Steppenwolf* the entrance is 'For Madmen Only', and the 'Price of Admittance Your Mind'. For those on the Path they pay with their longing for Truth, a longing which will take them beyond the conscious mind and the surface world of appearances, into the very depths of themselves.

In the fairground the dreamer enters a building, suggesting his own personal psyche, and what he wants is to find 'the deepest, darkest spot, from whence all trouble arose'. Thus the dreamer has an inner drive that directs him towards the darkest aspects of his psyche, and he knows the psychological truth that it is from the darkest spot 'that all trouble arose'. Just as Irina Tweedie's Sufi Master forced her 'to face the darkness within', so this man is shown in a dream how his Path is into the darkest place within himself. But first he went into different rooms in the building, exploring different aspects of his psyche. In some of these rooms he met a number of women and then he sees 'a very large, naked, white-skinned woman'. This latter figure is suggestive of the Earth Mother herself, vast and naked, and the women who proceed her are more personalised, less archetypal aspects of the Great Mother. Interestingly, when the dreamer gets closer and is 'face to face' with the naked woman, he finds her to be the same size as himself, and indeed notices that 'we somehow correspond'. The archetypal figures are only aspects of the psyche, and when confronted 'face to face' they lose their threatening proportions. Thus, when an individual consciously encounters the inner archetypal world, it can no longer dominate, or distort his perceptions. Yet the woman is still 'awe-inspiring', reflecting the very nature of an archetypal encounter.

But the dreamer does not stay with the Earth Mother, despite the 'slight erotic fascination' which would belong to a genuine meeting with this archetype. He has not yet found what he wanted, 'the darkest spot'. So he enters into a

corridor, where he meets two sinister men 'like KGB officials'. Russia is the shadow of the West, and thus the KGB
agents can be read as forces of repression that belong to the
shadow. However, the dreamer's comment, that 'they were
people who, like me, had come to this place, and could
never, ever leave it', makes a profound statement about the
psychological dynamics of the shadow. It would seem that
the shadow attracts aspects of consciousness that then
become imprisoned within its darkness, and finally become
the agents of the shadow. The dreamer's awareness that 'they
were lacking in some essential human attribute (possibly
love?) points to how the shadow acts, denying and negating
the humanity within the individual, until he becomes lost in
the darkness. Joseph Conrad's powerful study of evil, *The
Heart of Darkness*, explores this effect of the shadow in the
figure of Kurtz, who stayed too long in the primal world of
darkness, and losing his humanity became an agent of evil
and also its prisoner, a 'wandering and tormented thing . . .
irretrievably lost . . . a man . . . lying at the bottom of a
precipice where the sun never shines'. This is what the
dreamer rightly fears: that the KGB figures would 'remove
this same attribute from me', and then he would never be
able to escape.

The dreamer is not sure what this 'essential human attribute' is, but he thinks 'love'. The importance of love in
relation to the shadow is best imaged in the tale of *Beauty and
the Beast*, where the handsome prince is trapped within his
own shadow nature, the Beast, until this Beast is accepted
and loved for itself. For love is the most important human
quality; it alone can negate the primal power of darkness.

In *Beauty and the Beast*, Beauty must enter into the world
of the Beast for the process of transformation to take place;
similarly, our dreamer has to pass down a corridor and enter
into the inner world of darkness. There is also another
similarity, in that the house or castle in which the Beast lives
is surrounded by a forest, and the forest is often a symbol
for 'the realm of the psyche and the feminine principle',[14]
while our dream begins 'in a wild, swampy landscape',
which I have already suggested images the unconscious. It

would therefore seem that in order to meet with these inner figures one first has to traverse such an unknown inner landscape.

After passing down the corridor the dreamer then encounters 'the incarnation of evil', who is in fact 'a nondescript individual with glasses'. The identification of Satan as an ordinary man is a valuable comment on the nature of the archetype of evil, which is experienced by the individual as none other than the 'shadow', the ordinary, everyday aspects of himself which he does not like, and thus projects upon his neighbour. Jung writes:

> The devil is a variant of the 'shadow' archetype, i.e. of the dangerous aspect of the unrecognised dark half of the personality.[15]

In this dream the prince of darkness evokes great fear within the dreamer, 'the fear is greater than anything I have ever experienced'. For fear is the power of the shadow, the fear of the unknown, the fear of darkness. Furthermore, the intense feeling of fear experienced by the dreamer suggests that he had indeed encountered this primal darkness within himself; for the full affect of the archetypal world is experienced through its feeling tone.[16] In response to this fear the dreamer cries to God, which shows that within his psyche there is stamped a belief in that Higher Power which can 'lighten our darkness'. Indeed, he cries so loud that he wakes up his wife and daughter. And God responds to his cry by showing the dreamer 'the street a long way below and people walking about there, and, very vaguely, the contours of the building'. In this way God does not respond by removing the shadow figure, but by expanding the consciousness of the dreamer. Moreover, although this response did not offer any apparent solution, the dreamer himself was aware of its value, that 'it constituted a way out of this hopeless situation'.

First the dreamer is shown that, although alone in the room, he is not isolated; for as I mentioned, the power of the shadow is to imprison, to isolate the individual within himself and make him feel that there is nothing apart from the fear and darkness. A similar practice is used by interrogators when they isolate a 'suspect' and often keep him in darkness or semi-darkness, and then introduce the element of fear through the threat or use of torture, etc.

Once the individual is reconnected with a world outside darkness and fear, then the power of the shadow lessens. A similar result is achieved through the dreamer's seeing the outline of the building; for in this way he is shown the context of his experience, he sees the psychological situation that contains his meeting with the shadow. Once an individual is able to see the context of a psychological situation it becomes less threatening, and understanding can begin to dawn. It is always the unknown that is most frightening.

Thus, in calling out to God, to the Higher Powers within himself, the dreamer was able to see beyond his fear. He was not protected from the prince of darkness so much as given a more conscious perspective on the situation. For it is the light of consciousness that ultimately disarms the shadow, and allows it to be integrated as far as is possible.[17] But for this to happen the shadow must first be confronted, despite the intensity of feeling that can be evoked. The very act of meeting the shadow lessens its power, for just as the 'enormous naked woman' becomes the 'same size' as the dreamer when encountered 'face to face', so the shadow is seen to be 'an ordinary man I met this morning'.

In this dream there is also the interesting relationship between the shadow and the Earth Mother. Why, if the dreamer wants to find the 'very darkest thing' does he first meet the middle-aged women, and then the Earth Mother figure herself? Possibly the dreamer had a difficult relationship with his own mother, and thus the archetypal image contained aspects of the shadow. But he knew that this woman was not 'the darkest evil', and so there must be a deeper connection.

Within our Western culture the devil is associated with the dark aspect of the Feminine, in particular her sexuality. In *Genesis* Satan first persuades Eve to eat of the apple, who then 'gave also unto her husband with her; and he did eat'. And, as Christian culture developed with its spiritual orientation heavenwards, away from 'the lusts of the flesh', so the earth itself became associated with evil. Thus the devil became the 'activated darkness of matter, the *umbra Solis* (shadow of the sun)';[18] and the Earth Mother, *Mater Natura*, a corrupting force.[19] A relationship between the dark aspect of the feminine and the shadow is also suggested in many fairy tales. Indeed, in *Beauty and the Beast*, it was a witch who had enchanted the prince into the form of the Beast. But significantly, our dreamer, unlike many Puritan Church elders, did not see the Earth Mother as identical with Satan, and proceeded on his way to find 'the darkest evil'.

Central to the whole dream is the dreamer being driven by an inner urge to the prince of darkness, who is so frightening that the dreamer cries out to God. And here lies one of the mysteries of the Path, in that the Wayfarer is forced to confront the darkest aspects of his psyche, which can be so terrifying and overwhelming that his only recourse is to cry to the Beloved. In this way the shadow and all the inner difficulties are used like a ladder to take the Wayfarer nearer to Him. In great need you call out, and so He stretches out His hand and brings you closer.

The descent into the 'heart of darkness' contains another mysterious phenomenon which is that of the 'light in the midst of darkness'. In Christian symbolism this is the birth of Christ at about the winter solstice, and in the Taoist Yin-Yang symbol, it is imaged as the white point at the centre of the dark yin half (the dark point in the yang half points to another mystery, that of the darkness at the centre of light). Thus, the very search for the inner core of Darkness reveals the Light of God. The Self is hidden in the unconscious, and through the seeker's efforts towards reaching this 'subterranean centre' the Self unveils its secret: that it is his own essential nature. What this means in practice is that in each descent into the world of the shadow there comes an illumination as we discover more about ourselves, as we see more fully our own true self. And very gradually it dawns upon us that what we see is none other than the Self.

This dream pointed the dreamer in a definite psychological direction – towards the shadow and the archetype of evil. Psychological work is an important part of this Sufi Path, as reflected in the alchemical symbolism of the following dream. It was dreamt by a woman who at the time was wondering whether to come to our meditation group:

I am with people from the group and they are talking about making a sacrifice, but the sacrifice doesn't seem too difficult. Then I go to the next door room and there is an enormous fish full of light. I know that I have to merge with the fish and am worried, but then I look at my arms and see that I am made of the same a stuff as the fish.

At the core of this dream is the image of the 'enormous fish full of light'. Jung explored in some depth the alchemical symbol of the fish, which he understood as a content of the unconscious which is 'caught' or 'drawn out' from the depths. The fish is both the *prima materia*, the undifferentiated contents of the unconscious, and also the *lapis*, the end product of the alchemical process. For, just as the ox of the Zen 'Oxherding Pictures' is both the instinctual unconscious and also the divine Self, so the fish symbolises the unconscious contents which, through the process of transformation, become the alchemist's goal. The alchemical symbol of the fish can also be associated with Christian fish symbolism, again pointing to the psychological idea of the Self.

In our dream the size of the fish – 'enormous' – suggests the vastness of the unconscious which forms the psychic totality of the individual. Furthermore, the fact that the fish is 'full of light' indicates that it is indeed the Self, 'for the *lapis* is none other than the figure of light veiled in matter'.[20] The light of the Self is the light of divine consciousness that is hidden in the unconscious:

> Hidden in man, there exists such a heavenly and divine light which . . . cannot be placed in man from without, but must emerge from within.[21]

In Sufism this inner light is referred to as the 'man of light', the 'guide' who is the spiritual essence of the seeker. The 'man of light' is the Divine spark within the heart that 'gives birth' to the seeker, awakening him to the Path. And the Goal of the Path is to give birth to that same 'man of light', consciously to realise the Self. As in the dream of the man watching his own birth, there is the mystery that the 'man of light' is both the father and the child:

> Thou, my lord and prince, my most holy angel, my precious spiritual being. Thou art the Spirit who gave birth to me, and

Thou art the Child to whom my spirit gives birth . . . Thou who art clothed in the most brilliant of divine Lights . . . may Thou manifest Thyself to me in the most beautiful (or in the highest) of epiphanies, show me the light of Thy dazzling face, be for me the mediator . . . lift the veils of darkness from my heart.[22]

The dreamer knows that she must 'merge' with this fish, for it is necessary to unite with one's unconscious Self, as was imaged in a dream I discussed earlier when the dreamer 'became a buffalo'. Individual consciousness thus returns to the psychic totality from which it was born, not as a regression back into unconsciousness, but to effect the inner transformation that brings about the conscious realisation of the Self. Perhaps this is the 'sacrifice' that is being discussed at the beginning of the dream; for any such 'return' necessitates the sacrifice of the persona and one's conscious perceptions of oneself. For the dreamer 'the sacrifice doesn't seem too difficult', possibly because this process has already begun: 'I look at my arms and legs and see that I am made of the same stuff as the fish.' But for the Sufi the sacrifice of the persona is only a beginning, and is followed by many other sacrifices both painful and difficult, until finally the lower self, or ego, surrenders and merges into the Higher Self:

> The self will not go in gladness and with caresses,
> It must be chased with sorrow, drowned in tears . . .[23]

This dream of the fish has many similarities with the dream in which the man was watching the birth of his own child. Both dreams point to the birth of the Self and image the identification of the individual with that higher principle. But the dream of the fish places this spiritual dynamic within the context of alchemy, and Najm ad–din Kubra said 'Ours is the method of alchemy. It involves extracting the subtle organism of light from beneath the mountains under which it lies imprisoned.'[24] Alchemy provides a symbolic language for describing the psychological dynamics of the Path towards wholeness, and in the next chapter I will look more closely at dreams which image the alchemical *opus*.

4

THE ALCHEMY OF THE HEART
I – THE *OPUS*

> The goal is important only as an idea; the essential thing
> is the *opus* which leads to the goal: *that* is the goal of a
> lifetime (C. G. Jung).

Jung's first response to an alchemical text was 'Good lord,
what nonsense.' But later he realised the psychological
importance of alchemy, for he discovered that what the
alchemists were working with in their retorts and crucibles
were not just chemical substances, but the projected contents
of their own unconscious. The alchemical goal of turning
lead into gold was fundamentally symbolic, and referred to
the process of psychological transformation. The alchemical
opus is what we would describe as 'inner-work' or working
upon oneself, which aims to purify and transform the basic
contents of the unconscious. The alchemical 'gold' symbolises a state of inner transformation which relates to an
awareness of one's divine nature, what the alchemists called,
among other names, the *lapis*, or philosopher's stone, and
Jung termed the Self.

One of the important aspects of Jung's discovery was
that in alchemical symbolism there exists a language that
describes the processes of inner transformation. This transformation happens in the world of the psyche, which is a
world of images. Therefore, the language of alchemy is a
language of images, a language of symbols. Moreover, it is
a language that also appears in the dreams of individuals who
are engaged in their own inner-work. In this language the
unconscious communicates to the conscious mind, inform-
ing it of changes taking place in the depths. Through the

work of Jung we are able to revalue this almost forgotten, symbolic language of the psyche, and thus listen to and understand the voice of the psyche.

However, although Jung may have rediscovered this symbolic language for modern psychology, Sufis have always known about the inner processes of alchemy. A great twelfth-century Sufi, al Ghazālī, titled one of his most important books *The Alchemy of Happiness*. Moreover, the Arabic word for 'stone' is associated with the word for 'hidden, forbidden', and, according to the Sufis, the stone is the essence which is so powerful that it can transform whatever comes into contact with it. This relates to Jung's concept of the Self, and the idea that it is the philosopher's stone, the Self, that effects the whole process of alchemical/ psychological transformation.[1]

For the Wayfarer on the Path the process of alchemical transformation takes place fuelled by aspiration and meditation. And although one's spiritual journey is always a solitary path – it is the journey 'from the alone to the Alone' – the Sufi is in the hands of the Teacher and in the company of other Wayfarers, as is imaged in the following dream:

> The group is at a school for turning base metal into silver. The basic material is black earth which is swept up and sifted and finally a silver metal dust appears. We are all trying to make silver bowls from this stuff in our own way. Then I am taken aside and shown the secret way of doing this. You take a blank white sheet and spread the metal dust over the sheet five times. Then you clamp the sheet between two bowl moulds and squeeze. Then you take the rough bowl and polish and polish till it shines.

The alchemical process normally turns base matter, lead, into gold. But in this dream the 'base metal' is being turned into silver, which is significant in that silver is symbolically feminine; for it is the longing, the feminine side of love, the cup waiting to be filled, that takes the Sufi to God. This cup is the 'silver bowl' of the dream, which must be made in the workshop of the heart.

The dream's image of 'black earth' as the 'basic material' evokes the idea of the *prima materia*, which must be found before the alchemical process can commence. The *prima materia* is that which is rejected and considered waste:

> This Matter lies before the eyes of all; everybody sees it, touches it, loves it, knows it not. It is glorious and vile, precious and of small account, and is found everywhere.[2]

Psychologically, the *prima materia* is the undifferentiated contents of the unconscious that form the basis of the *opus* and is most often experienced in the form of unexpected moods or reactions. For at such moments, unconscious feelings express themselves; the unconscious 'spills over' into our conscious life. The alchemical process is concerned with the differentiation and integration of the unconscious, and therefore this process cannot begin without the individual 'getting hold of' the mercurial contents of his psyche.

Whenever one finds oneself reacting with more feeling or emotion than is justified by the objective situation, then something has 'come up' from the unconscious, and there is an opportunity to 'get hold' of the *prima materia*. It is, therefore, important to try to differentiate between what belongs to the external situation, and is an appropriate *response*, and what is primarily a *reaction*, something belonging to one's own unconscious patterns which have been 'triggered' off by the external situation. And because such unconscious material is not valued by the conscious mind, and is often considered humiliating, it is left lying around in the dusty corners of our lives, in unpleasant or humiliating incidents, where it can be found by the simple act of 'sweeping'. The *opus* commences by looking into those dusty corners and valuing what is found there, however disagreeable it may appear. The very act of taking notice of one's moods or reactions, and trying to understand their source, allows consciousness to begin to grasp and thus 'work' with the unconscious.

For most people today, the alchemical workshop is in the field of personal relationships. While the alchemists projected their unconscious into the mysterious processes of chemistry, we project our psychic contents most easily on to our relationships. Personal relationships form the groundwork for most analytic work, for it is here that we appear to have

least 'conscious control' of ourselves, and where the unconscious finds greatest room for expression. In fact, many
personal relationships are wrecked by the explosions of the
unconscious. Within our society, the nuclear family and the
importance attached to romantic love have placed immense
pressure on personal relationships, with the result that they
are often the battleground of the unconscious. Yet this
battleground can become a workshop for the transmutation
of the human being. It is in the feelings we project on to our
relationships that we have the most direct access to the
unconscious. Here lies the *prima materia* for the *opus* which
can be a human being's most important work. Here is the
'black earth' of the above alchemical dream which, when
swept up and sifted, becomes silver.

'Black earth' relates specifically to the first phase of the
alchemical process, the *nigredo* (*terra nigra*), which 'has its
parallels in the individuation process, in the confrontation
with the shadow.'[3] From a psychological perspective, the
work of transformation begins with the 'shadow', the repressed or unacknowledged parts of the psyche; and in
alchemy it is 'the black earth in which the gold or *lapis* is
sown like the grain of wheat'.[4] Therefore, just as for a
previous dreamer the Path began with the need to find the
'deepest, darkest spot' within himself,[5] so in this dream the
opus begins with sweeping up the 'black earth'.

However, 'sweeping' also has a specific Sufi symbolism,
for Sufis are known as 'sweepers' or the 'dustbins of humanity'. In one dream, Irina Tweedie met a Great Sufi with his
followers, and when she asked a disciple if he was a Bishop
she was told:

> 'No, no' . . . 'he is on the same line as Bhai Sahib [Irina
> Tweedie's Teacher], and he is very fond of joking: speaking of
> himself and those like him he will say: "Nous autres balayeurs"'
> (which means in French: 'we sweepers').
> 'Oh I see!' I exclaimed, 'it is because they clean the hearts of
> people!'
> 'Precisely!' the disciple said.[6]

And the idea of the Sufi as a 'dustbin' was reflected in a dream
told in our group:

I had two dustbins full of rubbish. The Teacher came along and emptied my two dustbins into his one dustbin, and walked off.

In this dream of turning base metal into silver, the dreamer is 'taken aside and shown the secret way of doing it': 'One takes a blank white sheet. Then you spread the metal dust over the sheet five times.' The 'blank white sheet' suggests purification, and corresponds in the alchemical process to the *albedo*, the 'whitening'. The 'whitening' is the light, the illumination that follows the darkness of the *nigredo*; for out of the confrontation with the shadow is born a purified state of consciousness.

That the metal dust is spread over the sheet five times is very significant, for five is the number of mankind or humanity: we have five senses, and in order to realise fully an inner transformation, it must be lived. This is reflected in the fact that, according to Jung, the final stage in the alchemical process, after the 'whitening', is the 'reddening':

> In order to come alive it must have 'blood', it must have what the alchemists call the *rubedo*, the 'redness' of life.[7]

On the Sufi Path this 'reddening' is effected through being 'in the world but not of the world'; and as I have already mentioned, a central feature of the Naqshbandi Path is 'Solitude in the Crowd', whereby the Wayfarer learns how to be involved in life, bring up a family, be a craftsman etc., and yet at the same time keep the inner attention focused on the heart. In this way the silver is spread five times, and then moulded by the grace of God from above, and by the experience of the world from below.

In this dream, the making of the silver bowl follows the three major stages of the alchemical *opus*, the *nigredo*, the *albedo* and the *rubedo*. But the 'rough bowl' made by this process should then be polished and polished 'till it shines'. This image of 'polishing' refers to the Sufi notion that the heart is a mirror which the Wayfarer polishes and polishes with his aspiration and longing, until no imperfection remains; then the mirror of the heart can reflect the True Light of the Beloved:

Whether your lot be glory or disgrace, be pure of both hatred and love of self. Polish your mirror, and perhaps that sublime beauty from the regions of mystery will shine in your breast – just as it did for the prophets. And then, with your heart illuminated by that splendour, the secret of the beloved will no longer be concealed from you.[8]

In this Sufi System the 'teaching' is reflected from heart to heart: the pure heart of the Teacher reflects the Truth into the heart of the disciple. Furthermore, being free of the lower self, the Teacher is also a mirror in which the Wayfarer sees his own nature reflected:

> O you who stab the selfless one with the sword, you are
>   stabbing yourself with it. Beware!
> For the selfless one has passed away, he has become a mirror:
>   naught is there but the image of another's face.
> If you spit at it, you spit at your own face; and if you strike the
>   mirror, you strike yourself;
> And if you see an ugly face in the mirror, 'tis you; and if you
>   see Jesus and Mary, 'tis you.
> He is neither this nor that: he is pure and free from self: he puts
>   your image before you.[9]

Thus the disciple is continually confronted with an undistorted image of his own nature, and is unable to escape the aspects of lower self that need to be worked on. In the mirror of the Teacher the disciple sees the blemishes of his own 'bowl', until finally this bowl is polished to such a degree that the Truth shines in it; and what he then sees is none other than a reflection of his own Divine Self. In the Sufi parable of the quest, *The Conference of the Birds*, when the thirty birds who had survived the journey asked their king and goal, the Simurgh, to 'reveal to them the secret of the unity and plurality of beings', the Simurgh made this reply:

> The sun of my majesty is a mirror. He who sees himself therein sees his soul and his body, and sees them completely. Since you have come as thirty birds, si-murgh, you will see thirty birds in this mirror. If forty or fifty were come, it would be the same. Although you were completely changed you see yourselves as you were before.[10]

THE PRIMA MATERIA

While the above dream describes the complete alchemical *opus*, the following dream focuses on the *prima materia*, which is imaged in a more ordinary, everyday context, though there is the figure of the Teacher helping the dreamer:

> I am in a room where there has been a party. There is a box full of all the left-overs from the party, crusts of bread etc. My Teacher tells me to eat the left-overs, but I don't know how to begin. I look at the box and think how can I eat all these things. My Teacher takes the box and a paper plate and arranges some of the left-overs in a nice pattern on the plate, and begins to eat – she shows how simple it is.

In this dream the *prima materia* is what is 'left-over' from the party of life. It is something undervalued and overlooked, rejected and considered inedible, which the Higher Self, personified as the Teacher, shows to be part of a pattern and so edible. Furthermore, 'she shows how simple it is', for spiritual life is in itself very simple, it is only the mind which would have us think otherwise.

Finding the *prima materia* is the essential first step in the *opus*, yet its definitions are vague and ambiguous. The following psychological situation and dream offer an example of 'getting hold' of the *prima materia*, and the transformative potential this offers:

> First I was aware of resentment towards my parents, and instead of just repressing it I decided to become more aware of it. This released a lot of energy and a dream followed:

> I was up a tower that was beginning to crumble, but I saw a vast, beautiful landscape. Then I went down the tower and was shown a large, gold eagle.

For a long time this man had been aware of his resentment towards his parents, and yet did not know what to do with it. From a practical perspective it is very difficult to know how to deal with such feelings. It is possible to express them, which in this case would mean for him to get angry with his parents. This can create a temporary release, but it is rarely a solution, and often inappropriate. For this man his parents would not have understood, or even been capable of understanding his resentment. Such feelings often originate deep in the unconscious patterns of the parents, which are then passed on to the children, stamped, or imprinted in the child's psyche. Thus a true understanding of a child feeling's towards his parents may require a depth of self-analysis and understanding that in many cases may be beyond the scope of the parents. Moreover, one cannot force someone else to become conscious. Jung commented that it can be totally inappropriate, even dangerous, to confront somebody with a psychological truth which they do not wish to or indeed cannot accept and integrate. Truth can be not only useless, but cruel, and 'when there is complete unconsciousness, don't say anything. The shock would be too great.'[11]

Faced with this predicament people often repress feelings that have no place in their conscious life; for what else are they to do with them? However, this man decided that he was no longer going to repress his resentment, and a dramatic psychological situation took place as he was cycling to work one day. Once again his feeling of resentment surfaced, but rather than repressing it, he decided to look at it, to become conscious of it. Suddenly, the whole energy flow in his body changed, and an enormous psychological shift took place. He had made the decision to work with the contents of his unconscious, in other words, the alchemical *opus* had begun. This actual decision in itself may have been the trigger that 'released a lot of energy', as psychic energy held repressed in the unconscious began to flow into consciousness.

'Awareness' is the most fundamental quality of consciousness, and in being aware of his resentment he formed a connection between consciousness and the unconscious through which the energy in the unconscious could begin to be integrated into consciousness. One of Jung's major discoveries was that the very process of being *aware* of the contents of the unconscious has a magical effect, vastly speeding up the transformative processes of the psyche. Jung believed that individuation actually happens to everyone,[12] but for most people it takes place only in the unconscious and is very, very slow. They hardly even realise that gradual changes are happening within them; changes that take them through the various stages of life and eventually prepare them for death. But the moment the individual becomes aware of what is taking place in the unconscious, then a spark of consciousness crosses over into the unconscious. It is as if this spark then ignites an immeasurably faster process of individuation, which is what we tend to refer to by the actual term 'individuation'. The participation of consciousness with the unconscious is like a chemical catalyst. This is when the *opus* really commences, and the dream that came when the man looked at his feelings of resentment offers a clear indication of the psychological process that he initiated.

The dreamer's tower can be read as a symbol of isolated consciousness, detached from the fundamental realities of life. This is echoed in the saying 'living in an ivory tower', with its implications of an unrealistic perspective on life. There is also a tarot card, 'The Tower of Destruction',[13] in which the tower images isolation and a state of psychological imbalance, cut off both from other human beings and also from the earth. A masculine symbol, it represents a mental construct that can serve as a protection against chaos, particularly the chaos of the unconscious; yet this tower often ends as a prison for its inhabitant. However, once an individual begins to acknowledge the world of the unconscious, and thus 'comes down to earth', any such tower will begin to crumble, which is what is imaged in this dream.

Moreover, the dreamer is shown two very auspicious symbols, 'a vast beautiful landscape' and 'a large gold eagle'. The 'vast beautiful landscape' is suggestive of new psychological horizons. Often in dreams there is the image of a new landscape, sometimes seen through a doorway, archway or window. For as we work upon the contents of the unconscious so there is an expansion of consciousness. The conditioning and complexes in which so much psychic energy is locked, are slowly worked upon and their energy released. Inner shadow-lands are explored and transformed, and these aspects of the psyche, rather than being locked in the darkness, are 'given a place in the sun' and become integrated into our conscious life. Thus in dreams people will find new rooms in their house, or even find a doorway to a whole new floor, possibly an attic which they did not know existed. And because the shadow not only contains the dark side of the ego, but also unlived potential, so that too becomes integrated, with the result that daily life becomes richer and more creative.

Psychological work is *real* and really changes a human being. We have become conditioned to believe that life can only improve externally, usually in quantitative, material terms: more is better. But meaning, and the richness that derives from life being meaningful, come from within. Real fulfilment comes from the inner and not the outer world; and deep psychological work results in lasting change that is not subject to the whims of fortune. As the inner darkness is transmuted, so more light comes into the psyche, and then the *quality* of life changes. External situations may change, as the individual discovers new potential that requires expression. But one's physical situation may also remain unchanged, and yet be perceived differently, just as we all know that the same street can be beautiful or nondescript depending on our mood. There is a Zen saying which expresses this truth about inner change,

> Before enlightenment, chop wood and carry water.
> After enlightenment, chop wood and carry water.

From the outside life may appear to be the same, but the experience is very different.

The dream of the crumbling tower has another symbol of transformation, 'a large, gold eagle'. The eagle, thought to be able to look unwavering into the full light of the sun, is a solar symbol, and in alchemy it signifies the philosophical gold.[14] Therefore the 'large gold eagle' images the transformation of the instinctual energy of the unconscious that results from working with the *prima materia*. This gold eagle is the same as the *lapis* which is both the beginning and the end of the *opus*. It is the spiritual principle within the dreamer that initiates the process, forcing him out of the tower and into contact with the unconscious. And this eagle is also the goal, his own divine Self which he will meet at the end of the Path.

THE FISH

Another alchemical symbol for both the *prima materia* and the *lapis* is the fish and it occurs in the next dream in association with the process of purification. This dream was dreamt by a woman after she had been coming to the group for nine months:

> I am cleaning out a fish tank, which has quite dirty water. There is a piece of mercury in the tank and I have to be careful so as not to disturb it. I had already taken out the fish, but while I am cleaning I find another fish which I put into the bath and have a bath myself with it. The fish then has babies and the bath is full of thousands of little fish.

'Cleaning out the fish tank' suggests the purification of the psyche, which is one of the most fundamental stages of the *opus*, primarily involving work on the shadow. The fact that the tank has 'quite dirty water' indicates that the shadow had polluted the psyche, which can easily happen if the conscious mind and the desires of the ego are the only focus of attention.

However, in the fish tank is 'a piece of mercury' and the dreamer has 'to be careful so as not to disturb it'. The presence of the mercury reinforces the alchemical context of the dream, for it alludes to the Spirit Mercurius, the spirit or God in matter:

> He [the Spirit Mercurius] is the spirit of the Lord which fills the whole world and in the beginning swam upon the waters. They also call him the spirit of Truth, which is hidden from the world.[15]

Jung explored the symbolism of Mercurius in detail,[16] and, like the *lapis*, it exhibits the paradoxical nature of the Self. The guiding principle behind the *opus*, Mercurius, is both its beginning and its end, and is thus similar to the 'man of light' who is both 'the father and the child'. Mercurius is the seed of Truth hidden within the heart of man that seeks to reveal itself. Yet it has an elusive nature, and easily disappears, leaving the Wayfarer feeling forlorn and lost. How often at first does that thin thread which is one's spiritual direction appear to have vanished, as outer circumstances and inner feelings fill the horizon. The dreamer is rightly aware that she has 'to be careful so as not to disturb it'.

While the dreamer is cleaning out her fish tank, she finds a fish which she hadn't noticed before, and she puts this fish into the bath and has a bath with it. This fish which had been overlooked suggests the *prima materia*, and in having a bath with it the dreamer personalises the alchemical *opus* that was begun by cleaning out the fish tank. For, while the fish tank is essentially separate from the dreamer, the bath images a process of more personal purification in which the dreamer participates with her whole body. Bathing is also an alchemical symbol pointing towards transformation, a transformation that requires the total involvement, or immersion, of the individual. Thus, the psychological work that was begun in a more projected manner as something outside of or separate from the dreamer, has now been internalised. For the *opus* often starts with an idealised goal, and gradually the individual becomes aware that the real goal is in the slow work upon oneself, '*that* is the goal of a lifetime'. Isabelle Rey, who worked with Jung for six months, expressed this same fact at the end of her time with him:

> I suppose I could express the finish by saying I did what I came to do, namely – touch the hem of Dr Jung's psychological garment – but it all seems so different now; I think I looked for a sort of spiritual baptism, which would insure protection and perfect understanding; instead it seems to me I have undertaken the tremendous responsibility of maintaining a standard of consciousness which is most difficult. I can never turn back, but God knows the prospect ahead isn't easy either.[17]

There is a Sufi story which tells the same tale, that although the inner journey may begin with a visible goal, the real Path is the work upon oneself. This is the *opus* which changes a human being:

> A father has several idle sons. On his deathbed he tells them that they will find treasure hidden in his field. They dig up his field and find nothing. So they plant wheat which provides an abundant crop. For several years they do this. They find no gold but indirectly they become both enriched and accustomed to

constructive labour. Ultimately they become honest farmers and forget the digging for gold.[18]

Once the individual begins to dig within himself, to work with the contents of the unconscious, then the alchemical transformation really commences and the unconscious reveals its fertility and abundance: in the dream the 'fish has babies and the bath is full of thousands of little fish'. The self-proliferation of this fish echoes the miracle of the loaves and fishes, and the fish can be seen as the 'miraculous food' of the eucharist 'drawn from the deep in order to nourish the needy ones of the earth'.[19] The fish is 'the nourishing effect of the unconscious', reminding the dreamer that all the necessary energy and understanding lies within herself, born from something humble and overlooked.

5

THE ALCHEMY OF THE HEART
II – THE INNER PARTNER

Each lover is alone, in secret, with the one he loves.
And I am here too: alone, hidden from all of them – With You.
(Rabi'a)

The alchemical *opus* begins with a process of inner purification, working upon the shadow. But behind the shadow
stands the animus or anima, the contrasexual aspects of the
psyche. For a woman, the animus is an unknown man who
is her divine lover, for a man, his dark lady is a goddess.
These mysterious figures are first known as the agents of
love, and through their magic attraction we fall in love and
are caught in the unconscious entanglements of romance.
They bridge the personal and archetypal worlds, and in them
we feel the fascinating power of the inner depths. Both the
animus and the anima have negative qualities which belong
to the shadow side of the personality; but they are important
inner figures, for, like Dante's Beatrice, they can act as guides
in the transpersonal realm. A good relationship with the
animus or anima is of great value, for it can help the seeker
on the spiritual path that leads beyond the ego to the Self.

However, Jung stresses that work on the shadow proceeds
any relationship with the animus or anima:

> the integration of the shadow, or the realization of the personal
> unconscious, marks the first stage in the analytic process, and
> without it a recognition of the anima and animus is impossible.[1]

In the following dream, this process is depicted. As in the
previous dream of the fish tank, it images inner purification
as an activity of cleaning, but what is born is a positive
relationship to the dreamer's animus, her inner partner.

I was cleaning a house with all the energy I had; I scrubbed, cleaned and polished every room until it shone. None of the rooms had doors and I was aware that on the floor of the main room in the centre of the house there was a man lying on a mattress on the floor and that he watched everything that I did. I was not disturbed by this but I just got on with my cleaning. My last task was to clean the toilet which was exactly opposite where the man lay. I put my heart and soul into this room in particular. The walls were tiled and I polished them so hard that I couldn't look at them; it was like trying to look straight into the sun. And then I noticed with horror that the window above the toilet was slightly open and I thought that some dust might fly in and that would disturb the man. Somehow I had to close the window, but it was extremely high up and there was no way I could reach it. I stood staring up at the window puzzling how I could close it when the man got out of his bed and came to me and put his arms around me. I thought how frail he was and yet what strength he had.

He reminded me of Ghandi to look at, and he said to me, 'From tomorrow I will share everything with you. If you have work I will share it. If the child cries in the night I will deal with it, and if you need love I will give you love.'

I felt as though a great burden had been lifted from my shoulders and I woke up thinking that this dream was about yesterday, today and tomorrow.

The dream begins with intense cleaning activity suggestive of work on the shadow, and in the centre of the house of the dreamer's psyche lay a man watching everything, yet not participating or helping the dreamer. She continues with her cleaning, finally putting her 'heart and soul' into cleaning the toilet and the tiled walls of this room. The toilet has psychological significance in that it is where one produces something out of oneself. It is a place of psychological creativity. Furthermore, the way the dreamer polishes the walls of the toilet adds a spiritual dimension to her cleaning, for it echoes the polishing of the mirror of the heart discussed earlier: 'I polished them [the walls] so hard that I couldn't look at them; it was like trying to look straight into the sun.'

However, a problem arose for the dreamer when she noticed that 'the window above the toilet was slightly open and I thought that some dust might fly in and that would disturb the man', and this window was too high up for her to close. The need to close the window could refer to the 'well-sealed vessel (*vas bene clausum*)' that is necessary for the alchemical *opus*. For the process of inner transformation requires that the contents of the psyche are hermetically sealed in order 'to protect what is within from the intrusion and admixture of what is without':

> Nothing enters into it [the stone] that did not come from it; since, if anything extraneous were to be added to it, it would at once be spoilt.[2]

Psychologically, this refers to the need to withdraw projections and to discriminate between what belongs to oneself and what belongs to another, for one can only transform the contents of one's own psyche, and the 'intrusion and admixture' of external psychological material leads only to confusion. In fact, this need for a 'well-sealed vessel' often results in a period of introversion as the individual withdraws from the outside world and 'broods' on the contents of his own psyche.

But, alone, the dreamer was unable to close this window, for the power of discrimination within the woman's psyche belongs to the animus. The animus provides the focus lacking in the 'diffused awareness' of the feminine mode of consciousness. Irene de Castillejo describes the animus as a 'torchbearer', 'holding aloft his torch to light my way':

> In a woman's world of shadows and cosmic truths he provides a pool of light as a focus for her eyes.[3]

Therefore, a positive relationship with the animus is necessary if a woman is to see the fine line that differentiates the contents of her own psyche from that which intrudes from outside.

Yet, as if in response to the dreamer's need for help to close the window, the male figure got off his bed and 'came to me and put his arms around me'. Frail and yet full of strength, he reminded her of Ghandi, who, according to Marie-Louise von Franz, often carries the projection of the highest stage of the animus,[4] the 'wise guide to spiritual truth':

> Finally . . . the animus is the incarnation of *meaning*. On this

highest level he becomes (like the anima) the mediator of the religious experience whereby life acquires a new meaning. He gives the woman spiritual firmness, an invisible inner support that compensates for her outer softness.[5]

And this inner support offered by the animus is most beautifully imaged in the words the male figure speaks to the dreamer, in which he is both the fellow labourer, the father and the lover:

'From tomorrow I will share everything with you. If you have to work I will share it. If the child cries in the night I will deal with it, and if you need love I will give you love.'

THE NAVEL OF GOD

The animus can give tenderness and strength, and also the inner clarity necessary for psychological work. The spiritual function of the animus is further portrayed in the following dream, in which it is through sexual union with a monk that the dreamer, a woman, is shown a spiritual dimension which she terms the 'Navel of God', symbolising a state of total dependence upon Him.

I am travelling with a monk, an unknown woman and another monk. We have travelled a long way. Then the scene changes and also the intensity of the dream, which becomes more real than real-life. I am in the monk's cell (somehow the other woman and monk have been absorbed into the background of the dream and are not visible). The room is very small, the ground is brown-red (a feeling of warmth). There is a simple pelisse on the floor and the monk and myself are lying on it, naked, embracing each other. I'm as white as the moon and he is slightly golden compared to me. The brown robe of the monk is hanging on a hook on the wall; otherwise the walls are bare. There is a deep sense of intimacy between us and also around us. I feel contained and supported.

I am an explorer and a 'God given person'. This is my name in the dream, and whatever act I perform with the monk will enhance this quality in me, the 'God given person'.

While we are making love my attention at one point moves to the area of his navel and belly. It is like absorbing and making a deep contact with that part of him, so I kiss and put my head there, and it is something so sacred and terribly important for me. Suddenly I move my head and remember something I had dreamt before, and I say to him 'I dreamt of the place that is the Navel of God and I need to go there.'

The monk says to me, 'I know that place and I will take you there.' Then he moves his hand and the place, 'the Navel of God', is in front of us like a vision in the room. It is a barren area of a yellow colour, sloping between two high, grey mountains. The sun is scorching, there is no vegetation. The vision is very powerful, almost dramatic, and I ask the monk what dress I will take to get there. I know I will have pink underwear but I have only an old Indian black dress. I have nothing else and I am frightened that the black colour will absorb even more heat from the sun. The monk smiles and he says, 'It doesn't matter. It will be terribly hot, but just enough that you can bear it.' I know that there will be a lot of wind as well before the scorching sun; and this whole vision powerfully contrasts the intimacy of the monk's cell. I look at the naked body of my companion with love and admiration. I know that his body is the map to find the Navel of God. Through his body we will find the place.

This profound dream begins with the image of the *quaternio*, two monks and two women, who have been travelling a long way together. The *quaternio* is a symbol of psychological wholeness, therefore the four travellers suggest that the dreamer has already reached a certain degree of integration, which is necessary for the union that follows to take place. But after this image the intensity of the dream changes and becomes 'more real than real-life', which suggests that it describes something of the greatest importance within the dreamer's psyche. The dreamer finds herself in the monk's cell, and he is 'her companion'. The monk is an aspect of the animus that gives a spiritual direction to the dreamer, leading her away from the world, towards God. The monk's cell, being 'very, very small', images this inner rather than outer orientation, and actually reflects the dreamer's real-life situation at this time, which had an ascetic quality as it was totally committed to her analysis and training as a therapist. Moreover, the details of the room, 'the ground brown-red (a feeling of warmth)', implies that this is not an idealistic venture 'up into the clouds', as such a spiritual withdrawal from life can often be. Brown is the colour of the earth, while red is the colour of blood; it images life-force itself. Thus this lovers' meeting is 'grounded' in the warmth of life.

The monk's cell also evokes the idea of the 'well-sealed vessel' alluded to with reference to the previous dream. This association is reinforced by the dreamer's life-style, which did not allow any external psychological influences, such as would come from a relationship, to interfere with her inner-work. As with the previous dream, the hermetic vessel within a woman's psyche directly relates to the animus, and for this dreamer the focus provided by her study and her male analyst enabled this state of containment to take place.

The hermetic vessel is a place of transformation, and this is imaged first by the inner union with the animus and then the visionary landscape, the Navel of God, revealed through him. The union of the couple takes place on the floor of the cell, and their naked bodies give it an archetypal quality, for she is 'white as the moon' while he is 'slightly golden', suggestive of the sun. Thus they symbolically enact the *coniunctio*, the mystic union of the masculine and feminine principles within the psyche, which is often depicted as the marriage of the sun and the moon. For the alchemists described the *coniunctio* not only as a chemical combination, but also as a marriage or love-affair in which the opposing 'natures' 'embrace one another'.[6] Moreover, the dreamer's feeling of being 'contained and supported' echoes the 'spiritual firmness and inner support' that Marie-Louise von Franz describes as an important quality of the animus, and that would be experienced through this union.

The dreamer describes herself as an 'explorer', for the integration of this animus figure gives her both the strength and the focus with which she can explore the inner world. And as much as in previous ages explorers charted unknown lands, the realm of the psyche is today still largely uncharted, and every venture into it is a voyage into the unexpected. For one friend spiritual life began in earnest when, after spending three years building a boat, she sailed, together with her husband and teenage children, from California to the Pacific Islands. During this voyage she realised that the outer world had already been explored, and the only real quest was within.

In the dream of the Navel of God, the spiritual dimension of the dreamer's quest is emphasised by her name in the dream, 'God given person'. This name suggests that all which comes to the dreamer is a gift from God; and while it is a Truth central to many religions that everything happens through God's Will, to live with this awareness as an inner reality and not just as a mental concept implies a state of surrender that is in itself an act of grace. But the essence of God's Gift to humanity is His own Divine Consciousness. This is His Greatest Gift, which Christianity symbolically alludes to in the phrase 'He gave His Only Begotten Son'; and it is this Gift which makes human beings the very 'crown of creation'. The aim of the alchemical *opus* is to find this 'Hidden Treasure', to realise that the very substance of our being is 'God given'.

However incongruous it might seem that a spiritual quest is furthered through making love to a monk, particularly with reference to the dreamer's own Catholic background, her unconscious tells her that 'whatever act I perform with the monk will enhance this quality in me, the "God given person"'. For just as everything that happens in life is to be accepted as a gift from the Beloved, so too does the dreamer see each act as an offering to Him. Thus, their embrace is a sacred act that will take her closer to her own Divine Nature; and as she makes love her attention 'moves to the area of his navel' which triggers something of great spiritual importance for her: '"I dreamt of the Navel of God and I need to go there."' The navel of the monk reminds her of a dream of the Navel of God, but what is significant is that this process happens through the body of the animus figure. It is when she kisses his navel and puts her head there that she remembers this dream, and later she says 'I know his body is the map to find the navel of God. Through his body we will find the place.' This points to the importance of her including the body in the spiritual process.

The relationship between body and spirit within a woman's psyche is very different to that within a man. For, while masculine consciousness, seeking to free itself from the unconscious world of the Great Mother, attempts to separate spirit from matter, within the consciousness of a woman these two 'opposites' are experienced as an integral part of one another:

> She understands, symbolically speaking, not with the head but with the whole body, in that her spiritual and corporeal processes are bound together in a way quite foreign to the average man.[7]

Thus the importance the dreamer attaches to the physical body of the monk, and the way that the 'Navel of God' is reached through his navel, reflects the feminine process by which the 'spiritual' is realised 'within the body'. As another woman was told in a dream, 'God becomes conscious in the body.'

The feminine principle itself is closely related to the world of matter, 'since time immemorial the feminine principle has stood for nature and matter – *Mater Natura*'.[8] Just as the woman gives birth and nourishes her children, so does the Earth. From Mother Earth are born all living creatures, and with her body she feeds them. They drink from her streams and eat the food she provides.

Therefore, because the archetypal feminine is so closely bonded with the earth, a woman's experience of her own feminine self will necessarily include the physical. In ancient matriarchal societies this integration of body and spirit was a part of the religious culture, embodied, for example, in the figure of the 'sacred prostitute', for whom sexuality and spirituality were undivided. However, this attitude was repressed by the patriarchy, and in Christianity only the body of Christ is sacred. The Catechism asks us to renounce the 'sinful lusts of the flesh',[9] and St Paul writes: 'Make no provision for the flesh, to fulfil the lusts thereof.'[10] As a result, the body and indeed the feminine principle itself have been rejected, repressed, and ultimately identified with evil. The alchemists, in their search for the light hidden in the depths of matter, sought to redress this imbalance, and today any quest for wholeness needs to embrace the physical. This is true for both men and women, but particularly so for women because in their very substance there is this sacred bonding of earth and spirit.

This dream emphasises the inclusion of the physical

dimension. Possibly this is a compensation for the Catholic
conditioning of the dreamer; but at the same time as
revaluing the feminine world of matter, it also stresses that
spiritual life is a love affair that involves the whole human
being; it even affects the very cells of the body. And finally,
when the lover is embraced by the Beloved, everything is
included:

> In the night, for instance, one is resting in God – body, mind,
> everything. The body is included – this is an important point;
> it too is resting in Him, and this gives such an experience of
> pure physical bliss. It is like relaxing within the endlessness of
> love . . .[11]

But what is this place, the 'Navel of God'? The dreamer's
immediate association was that the navel is where the umbili-
cal cord joins the body. It therefore suggests a quality of total
dependence in which one is fully nourished by God. The
phrase 'Navel of God' also evokes the association of the
'World Navel':

> . . . the symbol of the continuous creation: the mystery of the
> maintenance of the world through that continuous miracle of
> vivification which wells within all things.[12]

The World Navel is the symbolic place in the world which
is 'the source of all existence'. And while the origin of all
nourishment is the same One God, the difference between
the 'World Navel' and the 'Navel of God' is that the former
concerns life in this world, the abundance of the harvest, the
hearth in the home, while the latter reflects a spiritual
orientation in which the seeker looks only to God. Thus,
while the dream embraces the physical in the form of the
body of the monk, it also images an attitude of spiritual
renunciation.

The 'Navel of God' can be associated with the state of
'spiritual poverty' in which the pilgrim has nothing – all is
provided by Him. And because you want nothing but Him,
so you go to Him and remain with Him. This is the meaning
of Christ's saying in the Sermon of the Mount, 'Blessed are
the poor in spirit: for their's is the kingdom of heaven.'[13]

Even when living in this world, your attention is always towards Him. Whatever your outward activity, inwardly you are with Him, and nothing else matters. In his invaluable little book, *The Practice of the Presence of God*, Brother Lawrence describes such a state. Whatever Brother Lawrence did, he did with God: he peeled the potatoes with God, he cooked with God. Throughout his daily work, amid the noise and the clatter of the monastery kitchens, he remained always in an inner attitude of prayer, always in His Presence. There is a Sufi story about one of the Khwajas, or Masters of Wisdom, that portrays a similar state of spiritual attention, though with more dramatic outward consequences.[14] At the time of the Mongol invasion of Turkestan the Grand Master was Khwāja Arif Rīwgarawī. Rīwgara was a village about twenty miles from Bukhārā, and Chenghis Khān stopped there on his way to lay siege to Bukhārā. Most of the villagers had fled in terror, but Khwājā Arif was found by the Mongol soldiers working peacefully at his loom. Chenghis Khān was so impressed by his tranquillity and the skill of his work that, through an interpreter, he asked him why he had not fled in terror like all the other villagers. Khwāja Arif replied: 'My outer attention is on my work and my inner attention is on the Truth; I have no time to notice what is happening in the world around me.'

Chenghis Khān was so impressed with this reply that he ordered his soldiers to leave the villagers in peace, and asked Arif to go with him to Bukhārā and advise him whom he should trust. Unlike other cities which Chenghis Khān laid waste, the population of Bukhārā was not massacred.

In the dream of the 'Navel of God' the monk knows about such an attitude of spiritual devotion, for he says to the dreamer, 'I know that place and I will take you there.' Then he moves his hand and the place, 'the Navel of God', is in front of us like a vision in the room.

Once again the dream clearly states that her inner 'monk', the spiritual aspect of her animus, will lead her on her quest. 'The Navel of God' is imaged as 'a barren area of a yellow colour sloping between two grey mountains. The sun is scorching, there is no vegetation.' This barren land portrays the initial experience of becoming dependent upon Him, when everything seems empty and desolate and only the scorching sun fills the sky. After turning away from the world of Maya the painful process of purification begins, when everything is burnt away. For to renounce the world is not just to take up the orange robe of the Sannyasi, and say 'I have renounced the world.' Sitting on the banks of the Ganges, newly initiated Sannyasis repeat 'Ram, Ram,' and yet their eyes stray to the bodies of the Indian women bathing in the river below. As in a previous dream of a slave and a slave market,[15] although the chains of this world are made only of paper, they must be burnt away.

The dreamer knows that she needs to go to this empty land, yet the only dress she has is an 'old Indian black dress', and she is worried that the colour 'will absorb even more heat from the sun'. This may appear a practical consideration, but in Sufism the wearing of a black garment symbolises a state of renunciation.[16] Therefore, to put on a black dress is indeed to attract the fire of purification, though it is a spiritual law that we are never asked to bear more than we are able: 'It will be terribly hot, but just enough that you can bear it.' The scorching sun will burn away all her attachments to this world, leaving the dreamer empty . . .

> When does Gold Ore become pure Gold? When it is put through a process of fire. So the human being during the training becomes as pure as Gold through suffering. It is the burning away of the dross. I told you that suffering has a great redeeming quality. Like a drop of water falling on the desert sand is sucked up immediately, so we must be nothing and nowhere . . . we must disappear.[17]

For the woman, the animus is an important figure whose spiritual aspect can help her on the quest, allowing her to live from the sacred centre of her own being. Furthermore, a positive relationship with the animus as companion and lover leads finally to the inner marriage, the *coniunctio oppositorum*, that is the last stage of the *opus*. Within the psyche of the man the integration of the anima is of similar importance, though the anima has a different psychological dynamic to the animus. While the animus adds the strength and clarity of consciousness to the 'diffuse awareness' of the woman, the anima reconnects masculine consciousness to the inner world of the soul. For, unlike the woman who has never left the arms of the Great Mother, in his journey into manhood the boy becomes separated from the Source;[18] and with the help of the anima he can return to the depths of his own being without being lost in the maze of the unconscious.

The man's inner woman, the dark lady of the night, exerts her fascination in many guises, from the cover-girl to the enigmatic Mona Lisa. But whatever her form, she is the one who calls a man back to the centre of his soul, which, as much as it is the source of life, is the source of all true happiness. This quality of the anima is poignantly imaged in the following simple dream:

A woman in a slinky blue dress is singing 'Walking Back To Happiness' in a bluesy, soulful way.

The journey home is a long and painful path from the world of illusion to the world of Reality, but at the end of the road lies a happiness beyond any imagining. And just as the mother forgets the pain of giving birth when she holds her new-born child, so the sufferings of the Path dissolve in the Beloved's embrace.

6

THE REALM OF THE ARCHETYPES

> The archetype as an image of an instinct is a spiritual
> goal towards which the whole nature of man strives; it
> is the sea to which all rivers wend their way, the prize
> which the hero wrests from the fight with the dragon
> (C. G. Jung).

In the very depths of the psyche are the archetypes, the
primordial beings or energies that form the very basis of our
existence. They form the structure of the psyche. Revered in
the ancient world as gods, it is the archetypes which give
meaning to our individual lives – Jung called them 'determi-
nants of meaning'. And yet, over the past centuries, with our
belief in rationalism and our devaluing of the inner world of
the soul, we have forgotten about them, just as we have
forgotten about the importance of the symbolic images with
which they communicate with us. We are only just beginning to rediscover the meaning of this language of images,
we are just beginning to reconnect ourselves with these inner
gods. For these great beings or energies are a part of us,
and only need to be remembered and revalued for their
healing and transformative power to flow into our lives. Our
relationship to the archetypes can restore much of the sacred
meaning to life that for many people appears to been have
lost. They can help to heal our wounded world.

THE GODDESS

The spiritual path takes the seeker into the very depths of the
psyche, into the realm of the archetypes. The process of
transformation takes place not only in the personal uncon-

scious, the 'shadow', but in the realm of the archetypes. In the following dream the dreamer, a woman, encounters the Goddess, and yet is apprehensive of her power:

> I am in a circus, in the arena. There is a central post which holds up the tent. Many people are moving around the post, like in a merry-go-round. Then I see a woman who is very, very beautiful, the most beautiful woman I ever seen. She has stars on her ears and fingers. She is called Maria. Then in the middle of the arena there are some tigers. Maria and a male member of the group are quite happy playing with the tigers. Then the tigers go outside; but after a while they come back and I have to let them in. I see them first through a glass wall and am a bit apprehensive.

The dreamer meets the Goddess Maria in the circus arena, under the tent. The tent and its central post are ancient Sufi symbols, for the Sufi Teacher, the Shaikh, is the post, the link between heaven and earth which provides a protected space for the disciple to come closer to God. And in this dream the 'members of the group' are 'moving around the post, like in a merry-go-round', echoing the dream of the group on a fairground carousel,[1] and suggestive of the circular path towards wholeness. For the spiritual path is not a linear progression, the Truth is not separate from the seeker and the Path is a process of uncovering rather than 'getting anywhere'. I remember a dream in which, together with other members of the group, I was being led round and round in circles by the Teacher. In the dream there was a frustration about not going anywhere, but when I awoke I realised that there is nowhere to go:

> We shall not cease from exploration
> And the end of all our exploring
> Will be to arrive where we started
> And know the place for the first time.[2]

In the dream of meeting the Goddess Maria, the arena is a powerful symbol, for the Sufi, once committed to the Path, is taken into the arena to do battle with the *nafs*. And the words of the Roman gladiators, '*Ave, Imperator, morituri te salutant*' ('Hail, Emperor, those about to die salute you'), are appropriate to the Sufi, for in that arena the ego is to die, reflecting a saying ascribed to the Prophet, that one has to die before one dies. One can only realise the Truth when one has a physical body. Therefore, in order to reach Reality the ego has to 'die' before the physical body dies. This 'death' is not the obliteration of the ego, for one cannot live in this world without it. You need to have an individual identity to exist in the physical world, otherwise conscious life would be impossible: you would not know that you were separate from anyone or anything else. You and your neighbour would be the same, you and a table would be identical! Only in the states of Samadhi, in the *unio mystica*, does 'the ego disappear completely'. Then there is no individual identity, but a state of total oneness, as the individual is absorbed into the whole. However, in the arena the ego is dissolved and transformed so that it remains constantly surrendered to the Higher Self and to God. For the disciple this transformation is experienced as a death, a painful process of dying to this world and its desires, in order that one may fully awaken to the presence of the Beloved.

There, in the arena, the dreamer meets the Great Goddess, known in the West as Maria, or the Virgin Mary. 'The most beautiful woman I have ever seen', she is adorned with stars, reflecting her archetypal nature, and she is playing with tigers. The tiger is a vehicle of the Goddess,[3] and is often associated with her dark side, the Terrible Goddess. The tiger represents her power, her undifferentiated primordial energy, which is the aspect of the Goddess most repressed in our patriarchal culture. It is a quality of the Goddess which is both beautiful and terrible, as is encapsulated in Blake's poem, 'The Tyger':

> Tyger! 'Tyger! burning bright
> In the forests of the night,
> What immortal hand or eye
> Dare frame thy fearful symmetry?

This is the primal power of the feminine of which men are most afraid. And in this dream the power of the goddess is emphasised by there being more than one tiger. Moreover,

it must be integrated by the dreamer, 'I have to let them in.'
Understandably, she is 'a bit apprehensive'. She is frightened
of her own feminine power.

The deeper one goes in the unconscious, the more one has
to accept and integrate the energy that is there. And this
energy places an ethical obligation upon one. The archetypes
belong to the amoral depths of the unconscious. Just like
tigers in the jungle, they are awesome but impersonal forces
of nature, each following nature's amoral and impersonal
laws. It is for the consciousness of the individual to add the
dimension of ethical, human values to these numinous
entities. Then the energy of the unconscious may be integrated
beneficially, rather than swamping or distorting consciousness with raw power.

The ethical responsibility demanded by the images of the
unconscious is reflected in a more personal dream which
followed this archetypal dream. It illustrates the subtle inter-
relationship between the collective and the personal unconscious, showing how an experience of an archetype required
her to look closely at an aspect of her shadow:

> There are two men, one of whom wants to use me as a
> prostitute. I don't really want to, but an unknown woman is
> there who says that it is O.K.; she often does it, she just thinks
> about something else.

Portrayed in sexual imagery, this dream describes a personal conflict within the dreamer, and one that is also a
central part of our patriarchal culture: the woman allowing
herself to be used by a man. In this dream there are two men
and two women, suggesting the marriage *quaternio*, yet in
this case the sexual union would not represent integration,
as the woman is being 'used'. It is appropriate here to refer
to Esther Harding's understanding of the term 'virgin':

> The term virgin, when used of the ancient goddesses, clearly has
> a meaning not of today. It may be used of a woman who has
> had much sexual experience; it may even be applied to a
> prostitute . . . A girl belongs to *herself* while she is a virgin . . .
> she is 'One in herself'.[4]

Rather than belonging to a man, a virgin, with or without sexual experience, belongs to the Goddess, to her own feminine self.

Similarly, the image of prostitution in this dream refers to a woman denying her own feminine self for the sake of a man, or the masculine; she does not respect the Goddess within. Significantly, it is an 'unknown woman', a shadow figure, who 'says it is O.K.' and 'often does it' without being fully aware of what she is doing, 'just thinks about something else'. As ever, the shadow acts unconsciously, and here suggests that the figure of the dreamer should do likewise. The shadow often tries to limit our conscious awareness, and pull us into its murky world. And because it is a part of us, it knows the easiest way to do this. The shadow knows our weak spots.

When discussing this dream, the dreamer wanted to know what to do, and it was suggested that she should just become aware of her relationship to the masculine as imaged in this dream; rather that thinking 'about something else' she should become conscious of that part within herself that sacrificed her feminine integrity to the masculine. A few days later she had a dream in which a tiger came and licked her face! After encountering the Goddess, the dreamer had to respect her feminine self, the Goddess within her; no longer could she prostitute herself. But in being aware of that tendency within her she was no longer apprehensive of the power of the Goddess: the tiger came and licked her face. In order to integrate this primal power and use it creatively one must become conscious of the shadow, for the undifferentiated energy of the unconscious is only dark and frightening when it manifests through the shadow.

I find that this series of dreams offers a profound insight into the relationship between the archetypes and the shadow. This dreamer was able to transform her relationship to the Goddess through becoming aware of an aspect of her shadow. Furthermore, while our culture conditions us to think that results are only achieved through 'doing something', the final dream shows the effectiveness of just becoming aware.

Interestingly, the desire to 'do something' is a masculine drive, while inner realisation is the result of a feminine approach, one which echoes the Way of the Tao: 'work without doing'. Furthermore, Sufism, like Taoism, is a feminine Path, a surrender to the unknown. The feminine nature of the Sufi Path is very advantageous when working with the unconscious, for this work requires a particular mode of awareness that Neumann calls 'matriarchal consciousness'. Matriarchal consciousness is a receptivity to the transformative processes of the unconscious that allows the meaning of its symbols to be realised in their wholeness. It is being aware and attentive to the images and feelings of the unconscious, rather than 'doing anything'. Unlike patriarchal, ego-orientated thought, matriarchal consciousness works in harmony with the unconscious, and as opposed to the 'coldness' of abstract, analytic thought, it includes feeling. Neumann says it belongs symbolically, not to the head but to the heart, and it is a process of 'brooding' that is necessary for understanding the meaning of the symbolic world.

> Processes of growth are processes of transformation . . . Matriarchal consciousness mirrors these processes and in its specific way accompanies and supports them . . . Matriarchal consciousness experiences the dark and mysterious process of growing comprehension as something in which the Self functions as a totality.[5]

MYTHOLOGICAL THINKING

Neumann's 'matriarchal consciousness' and its relationship to the more ego-orientated, systematised 'patriarchal consciousness' is best understood as analogous to Jung's 'mythological' and 'directed thinking'. In *Symbols of Transformation* Jung distinguished between two types of thinking, which can be equated with the thinking processes of the left and right cerebral hemispheres of the brain. 'Directed thinking' belongs to the left side of the brain. It is logical and allows for thinking in words; it also develops with the acquisition of language; it is analytic and allows for abstract thought. Fundamentally directed towards the outside world, it is the development of this mode of thought that has resulted in the achievements of science and technology.

Jung's 'mythological thinking' is related to the right side of the brain. It is holistic rather than analytic; it does not attempt to dissect or rationalise; rather than thinking in words it thinks in images; and as opposed to the more masculine, active, idea-forming process of the rational mode, is primarily receptive, 'observing the change and development of its images'. *It allows for the formation of symbols, and as such, a symbolic relationship to life.* It can be seen at work in dreaming or in the progression of fantasies. As the thinking process of the unconscious, it is the elder of the two modes, belonging, according to Neumann, to the Matriarchal era of human consciousness. It is fundamentally subjective, pre-verbal and mythological. Jung gives an example of its functioning, and also compares its 'goal' with that of 'directed thought':

> The activity of the earliest classical mind was in the highest degree artistic, the goal of its interest does not seem to have been to understand the world as objectively and accurately as possible, but how to adapt it aesthetically to subjective fantasies and expectations.[6]

However, this mythic mode of thinking has been suppressed in Western, patriarchal civilisation by the increasing dominance of 'directed thought'. Indeed, recent neurological research has shown that the thinking process of the left hemisphere can actually repress and inhibit the right hemisphere, in particular its emotionally toned activities.[7] Along with many aspects of the feminine, 'mythic thought' has been devalued and for the majority it exists unrecognised in the unconscious, expressing itself only in dreams, fantasies and vague feelings. If we are to explore and understand the depths of the unconscious, and in particular the archetypal realm, we need this mode of thinking, this feminine perception.

The symbolic world requires an attitude of *receptivity*, only then can its transformative potential be realised. For the symbols of the psyche act as transformers of psychic energy. They transform the undifferentiated energy of the primal depths into a form that can be integrated into consciousness. In this sense they are like electrical power stations which transform high-voltage current into voltage that can be of domestic use. In previous eras religious symbolism had this function, for example the Christian symbolism of the Mass, through which the energy of the archetypal world could be 'eaten' and 'drunk' by ordinary people. However, it appears that the relationship between individual consciousness and the archetypes is changing. For many people the collective symbols of a religion no longer act as true transformers of psychic energy. They no longer have a numinous attraction, but have lost their meaning. Instead there is an increasing need for people to find their own individual relationship to the archetypal world, to discover their own symbols, their own personal myth.

If we are to form our individual relationship with the archetypes and work with their symbols, we need to learn to create an inner space in which such symbols can manifest. At a time when I was beginning to work with the depths of the unconscious I had a dream which beautifully illustrated this. It acted as a guide that never failed:

> I was with my Teacher, who asked me to go and get him an Easter Egg. I went into the town and looked everywhere, but couldn't find it. I went back to where I had left the Teacher, but he wasn't there. Someone told me that he couldn't wait.

When I awoke from this dream I felt very upset. The one time my Teacher asked me for something I couldn't find it, and not only that, but he couldn't wait. Then suddenly I understood: it was not the Easter Egg he wanted, but the space in the middle, Easter Eggs are made of very thin chocolate, and are mainly an empty space! So in working with the unconscious I tried always to keep an empty space, and to be very attentive to the images and feelings that evolved.

THE INNER SECRET

On the Path, the psychological and the spiritual work

together, for just as one creates an inner space for the symbolic world, so one creates an inner space for Him. Learning to listen within to the unconscious is also learning to listen within to Him. One important psychological effect of the feminine nature of the Sufi Path is that 'the whole process takes place through the unconscious', as was imaged in a previous dream in which the dreamer had a gold ring placed around her left foot.[8] Just as the *opus* begins in the darkness of the *prima materia*, so the spiritual transformation of the Sufi takes place in the depths of the psyche, and often only comes to consciousness in its final stages. This is movingly imaged in the following dream:

> I suddenly found that I was giving birth, and there wasn't a doctor or a midwife there, only a woman who had already had children. I saw the head of the child beginning to come out, and I knew it was going to be very painful, might even rip me apart, but the only thing I could do was think of what it would be like to cuddle the baby when it was born.

In an earlier dream a man saw the birth of his own child, pointing to the birth of the Self. Here the dreamer is a woman and she is aware that there is no doctor or midwife to help her give birth, 'only a woman who had already had children'. All that is present to help the dreamer in this process is the part of herself that has the natural wisdom of experience. If the child being born is the dreamer's divine nature then the woman 'who had already had children' would be the archetype of the wise old woman, who over the aeons has brought this child into the world countless times; and can thus provide all the wisdom and understanding that is needed.

However, the child is not yet born. The dreamer only 'saw the head of the child' suggesting that this inner process is only just becoming manifest. As I have already mentioned with reference to the image of the arena, the birth of the Self is a very painful process, as it involves the 'death' of the ego. In Christian terminology this is the crucifixion, and so the dreamer is right to think it 'might even rip me apart'. The Sufi says that two cannot live in one heart, either the ego or the Beloved, and for the ego to go it must be 'chased with tears'. Yet the dreamer will bear this pain, for she keeps her attention on her feelings of love for the One who truly belongs in her heart, 'the only thing I could think of was what it would be like to cuddle the baby'.

The beauty of this dream is that it describes the most profound inner change in the simplest human imagery. Just as the greatest human miracle is the birth of a child, so too is the greatest mystery of the soul a simple birth. Moreover, the dreamer 'suddenly found that I was giving birth'; she was not even aware of being pregnant, for the whole inner transformation that leads up to this moment happens silently within the soul. The Sufi Path is a secret affair of the heart, and sometimes this is so secret that it is hidden even from the knowledge of the lover.

The fact that the Wayfarer is often unaware of the process of inner transformation also serves a spiritual purpose, for only too easily can the ego identify with any 'progress'. This is reflected in Irina Tweedie's thoughts about asking her Teacher to be initiated as his disciple:

> It would be in contradiction with what I am trying to do, namely, grappling with the gigantic task of learning how to become nothing. If I ask him to become something, his disciple, that would be a limitation.[9]

Therefore, as the aim of the Sufi is to transcend the ego – indeed a great deal of the Sufi's energy is directed against the *nafs* – the less that he knows about the true stage of his development the better. This is an idea that can be traced back to the ninth-century Sufi of Nishapur, Abū Ḥafs al-Haddād.[10] Abu Hafs believed that the only way to stop the ego taking a share in any spiritual experience is to internalise the process to such a degree that the ego does not know anything. Therefore, he taught that one cannot do anything if one is in the public eye. For if the public identifies one as a mystic or a Sufi, someone who has spiritual experiences, it would be impossible to escape the ego also becoming identified with the spiritual process.

In the ninth-century most Sufis could be distinguished by their 'patched frock', or by the fact that they lived at times in a special 'monastery' or 'ashram', '*zawiya*'.[11] Moreover, they practised their meditation in what used to be called 'spiritual concerts', 'sama', which included music, dancing and sometimes a special singer. Thus, Abu Hafs and the Sufi circle in Nishapur adopted two methods that four centuries later were to become the basis of the Naqshbandi Path. First they believed in not appearing different from 'ordinary' people, an attitude which was to become formulated as 'Solitude in the Crowd';[12] and second they practised 'silent meditation'. In fact the essence of 'silent meditation' is that even the mind does not know anything, for 'What can be understood by the mind is not a high state'. This whole approach is reflected in the following dream, which is probably not a dream at all, but an experience in the night:

> I am with many people dressed in long white robes, but I am in ordinary dress and feel out of place. A report is being given to the assembled company about my spiritual development, but I have been made deaf so that I shall not hear it.

The dream of the woman watching herself give birth, together with the dream of the man watching his own birth, could be mistakenly read as implying that the birth of the Self is a momentous event occurring at a particular time in the life of the seeker. Yet the process of inner awakening not only happens gradually, but it also manifests in stages as consciousness slowly expands. 'Enlightenment' is simply an expansion of the horizon: for a baby its mother's breasts and then the cot are the whole world; slowly, the house or apartment becomes the child's world, and then school and the neighbourhood. Just as the child's world slowly expands, so does the spiritual world of the seeker. But the absolute knowledge of Brahma, *Brahmavidya*, is infinite, and so too is the Path to Enlightenment: 'What is the Goal? For a thousand years you can go on, and it recedes.'[13]

The Spiritual Path is an infinite journey across a shoreless ocean. It is a continuous process of discovery as the horizons of the heart open and open. Like climbing in a great range of mountains, after struggling and struggling you reach one peak, only to see that beyond you there is another, higher peak. And always the mystery deepens, the awe and wonder increase. This is a journey that never began and will never end. Meister Eckhart said 'God is the sigh in the soul', and we all carry that sigh deep within us, we brought it with us from far, far away. The spiritual journey takes us back to the source of this sigh, into our very heart of hearts.

It is a journey Home, and yet, paradoxically, each step on the Path is a venture into the unknown. In the following dream this is imaged by the dreamer jumping off an escarpment:

> I am walking along an escarpment and I come to a point where I can only go on by jumping off. I jump off and there is a space of four days. Then I am on a hillside full of flowers, and there are some footprints which are my father's, though it is not a personal father. My father is further up the hillside. I walk up the hill carefully putting my feet in the footsteps of my father.

How often on the Path does one reach a point where one 'can only go on by jumping off'? Each major unfolding within is only realised by leaving behind the patterns of the past, and for the Sufi the twin qualities of faith and surrender are fundamental. For, whatever the doubts that trouble the mind, it is only through faith that one surrenders into the unknown. And this faith comes from the remembrance that one belongs not to this world of forms, but to the world of the spirit, as is beautifully illustrated in the story of the stream:

> There was once a stream that flowed through many lands until it came to a desert. It could go no further. There was no way for it to cross the desert. Its waters just disappeared into the sand. Yet the stream felt in the depths of its being that it was to cross the desert. Faced with what seemed an impossible situation the stream was on the point of despair, when a still, small voice whispered in its ear, 'In your present form you will never cross the desert. But although to you it seems an impassible barrier, the wind crosses the desert, and so can you. If you surrender into the arms of the wind, and lose yourself within it, you will be lifted over the sands. Then you will fall as rain, and become a stream again.'
>
> But the stream did not like this idea. It had never lost its own identity before. And once this was lost, could it ever be found again? Would the stream not simply disappear forever?
>
> Again the voice spoke to the stream, 'I know that you have

doubts, but do you have any alternative? If you remain in your present form you can go no further. You may think of yourself as a stream, but that is not your true essence. If you surrender to the wind your essence will not be lost.'

These words echoed within the stream, and awoke distant memories that long, long ago, some essential part of itself had been borne in the arms of the wind. With this memory came the realisation that to surrender to the wind was the only thing to do. Its true self would not be lost. It could never be lost.

And so the stream surrendered into the welcoming arms of the wind, which lovingly absorbed it, and carried it over the desert and far away, until it reached some distant mountains, where it fell as rain. And because it had had its doubts, the stream was able to remember this whole experience, and in doing so it realised its true identity.

Like the stream, our dreamer can only go on by leaving behind what is known. And although he does not cross a desert, there is a similar quality of emptiness in the 'space of four days' that lies between his jumping off the escarpment and finding himself 'on a hillside full of flowers'. Furthermore, just as the stream was able to realise its 'true identity' through surrendering to the wind, so the numerical significance of the 'four days' points towards wholeness and integration; and the flowers on the hillside could indicate a new flowering within the dreamer.

However, the psychological context of this dream is given by the 'footsteps which are my father's, though it is not a personal father'. In jumping off the escarpment, the dreamer has been able to find in the depths of his psyche the archetypal father-figure. This is the archetype that carries the masculinity of a man, uncontaminated by the personal father. Normally, the personal father carries the masculine energy of the archetypal father, and thus a boy realises his own masculinity through his relationship with his father. But if the father is absent, or due to limitations of character cannot carry the archetype of the father, then his son must discover his own masculine identity either through another father-figure, or a direct relationship with the archetype itself. This dream points towards the latter; in leaving one land the dreamer has left the world of the personal father, to find on a hillside full of flowers the footsteps of the archetypal father. At present the dreamer has not yet reached the archetypal father, who is 'further up the hillside'; he must still climb further. But he is able to walk in his footsteps, in other words, live in tune with the imprints of his own archetypal masculinity.

This encounter with the archetypal father was reflected in a personal experience which I had when trying to realise my own masculine identity. My personal father was never able to carry the projection of the archetypal father, and so there was a period when I was seeking for a father-figure, someone who was both strong and understanding. However, these projections necessarily failed, and eventually I became aware of this dynamic and realised that I could never find this father-figure outside of myself. As with most processes, there was a situation which finally triggered this realisation: I went to meet a man whom I hoped would understand and help me with some work I had been researching, and I saw that I was projecting far more into this meeting than it warranted. Once again, I was searching for a father-figure, and I got so fed-up with this repetition that I consciously withdrew the projection. I had an enjoyable meeting with this man without any unconscious expectations or disappointments, and when I arrived back home I found that the television had been left on and it was showing a nature programme about the life of a stag. The film had just reached the point in the young stag's life when he returned to the herd to challenge and defeat the ruling stag. Only when I awoke the next morning did I realise the synchronistic implications of this programme. Within myself a natural cycle had been completed in which I had claimed back part of my own masculine identity from the unconscious.

Yet any relationship with an archetypal figure demands a sacrifice: I had to give up my quest for a father figure, just as the dreamer had to jump off an escarpment. In the following dream the dreamer – a woman – meets the masculine archetype of the wise old man, but first she is left behind, alone:

> In the town where I grew up, a coach full of all the people I knew leaves without anyone saying goodbye. Following it is a truck with all my luggage. I am left alone on the pavement with nothing but my handbag. An old man comes to whom I owe £10. I open my bag which is full of paper money and give him £10.

Back in the place of her childhood, the dreamer witnesses the departure of her conditioning, 'all the people I knew'. These people image the environmental, educational and parental influences of her childhood: influences that conditioned her into certain conscious and unconscious patterns of behaviour and values etc. The fact that they leave without saying goodbye points to the fact that there is no longer any real relationship between the dreamer and the world of her past. Furthermore, they take with them a truck full of all her luggage, indicating that she is now free of many psychological encumbrances.

In freeing herself of her personal conditioning, the dreamer is able to form a relationship with the archetype of the wise old man, who appears now that she is left alone on the pavement. For just as Jung stresses that a confrontation with the shadow must precede any real meeting with the animus or anima, so too an individual needs to have left behind much of his personal conditioning before there can be a direct relationship with the archetypal world. The figures of the collective unconscious have a very different outlook on life than that encompassed by our conditioning. Theirs is a deeper and more ancient world that moves according to different rhythms which encompass both past and future aeons, while our conditioned perception looks back only to our childhood. Thus, while the previous dreamer had to jump off into space before he could find the footsteps of the archetypal father, and I had finally to give up the hope of a personal father-figure before I could realise that same archetype, so in this dream the departure of 'the coach full of people I knew' creates a space for the old man to appear. Yet the dreamer owes this old man £10, which suggests that she needs to value this archetypal figure, and this is what she does; for although all her luggage has gone and she has been left with nothing but her handbag, this handbag is full of money. Once the psychological clutter of her conditioning has gone, the dreamer has access to her inner wealth and is able to appreciate the importance of this archetypal figure.

While this dreamer was left with her handbag, for another dreamer, meeting with an archetypal figure was preceded by the loss of his wallet:

> I have lost my wallet which includes a filo-fax; however, I am not worried. A man dressed in black like a priest comes and gives me a wallet of old leather, but inside there are no pages. It is empty except for star-dust and a few flowers. I take the wallet and the man goes, and I am then in a skyscraper which has no door or windows, but the sunlight streams in from above.

The loss of this dreamer's wallet and filo-fax points to the loss of a certain identity and psychological structure, for a wallet contains money, credit cards and other forms of identity, while the filo-fax is a contemporary means of structuring and ordering one's life, as well as being a 'yuppie' identity symbol. Yet the dreamer is not worried, presumably he is not too attached to these values and is thus able to give them up. Nevertheless, they indicate a personal conditioning which has to be lost, before there can be a shift to a more archetypal perspective on life.

The man 'dressed in black like a priest' has an archetypal rather than personal quality, and he gives the dreamer a wallet of old leather that 'is empty except for star-dust and a few flowers'. The stars have always imaged for mankind the divine realm of the Gods. They have carried the projection of the inner world of the soul, and astrology is the ancient science of the psyche, charting the interplay of the psychic forces that Jung termed archetypes. Thus, this ancient archetypal figure replaces the contemporary filo-fax with a symbolic reminder that the dreamer is not just made of the dust of the earth, but has a divine soul, which, according to myth, came from the stars and will return there after his death.[14] Moreover, stars have often acted as guides, whether for mariners on the sea or the Magi searching for the birthplace of the new King. They direct our attention away from the seeming chaos and confusion of our world, towards the realm of eternity; and there is a belief that at birth each person is given a guiding star which watches over his destiny. This guiding star is the light of the Self burning in the heart of the human being, and it is the one true guide we each have.

Besides the stardust, the old leather wallet also has a few flowers which echo the flowers on the hillside of the dream of the father archetype. These flowers suggest that if the dreamer lives not just in the surface world of today, but also in contact with and guided by the eternal world of the soul, a flowering can take place. And the flowering of the soul is a process both beautiful and natural. It is the birthright of man.

When the dreamer takes the wallet, a transformation takes place and he finds himself 'in a skyscraper which has no doors or windows but the sunlight streams in from above'. Thus the orientation of the dreamer is firmly directed away from a horizontal, temporal perspective, towards the vertical and the eternal. Just as the soaring arches of the Gothic cathedrals turn one's attention upwards, to the heavens, so the dreamer must look up to where the sunlight streams in. The stardust is working its magic, and light only enters from above. The dreamer's psyche is therefore, illuminated from the very centre of his being, by the sun that is our world's star.

THE MYSTIC MARRIAGE

Someone asked Junaid: 'Slave of God who yet are free,
tell me how to reach a state of contentment?' Junaid
replied: 'When one has learned through love, to accept'
(*The Conference of the Birds.*)

'As above, so below' is an ancient alchemical saying, describing how the inner world mirrors the outer. The psyche is as vast as the heavens, and the stars in the night sky are reflected in the archetypal realm. Within us we stretch to unknown depths, and there, in the deepest and darkest place lives the serpent. Together with the dragon, the serpent is an ancient symbol for the primordial power of the whole psyche. In the dream of the lover and the serpent,[1] the divine lover touched the dreamer in the depths of her heart. The dreamer then felt a tongue in her mouth, and opening her eyes found that she was embracing a serpent. This dream imaged the fact that the Path of Love takes the Wayfarer into the innermost depths. Not only must the shadow, the dark side of the ego, be embraced and integrated, but also the deepest layers of the collective unconscious.

At some stage on the Path the great snake must be encountered, for only then can the individual fully transmute the energy of the unconscious. But how is such a primordial power to be approached? In the following extract from a longer dream, the dreamer is shown by a teacher figure how the serpent can become a friend:

> I visited a swami who had a building of two circular structures on different levels. I followed him to the upper level, where there were a number of his male disciples around a pool. The swami went into the water, and in the water was his beloved

serpent. I was kind of merged with the swami, was in him in the water, and I was quite frightened by this huge snake, but he wasn't. He told me that the snake was his great friend because he had surrendered to the snake, and it didn't kill him because he had surrendered to it. The snake was his friend because he had accepted it.

In the dream discussed at the end of the last chapter, where the dreamer lost his wallet, the archetypal world was imaged as stars, offered to the dreamer by a priest figure. In this dream the same primal world appears as a serpent, which a similar religious figure, a swami, introduces to the dreamer. For just as the descent into the depths of the psyche is equivalent to the ascent to the realm of the soul, so the serpent of the depths images the same psychological dimension as the stars above. Moreover, for any venture into this imaginal interior it is necessary to have a guide in the form of the wise old man or woman, or teacher figure. One needs a guide to cross an unknown land, and the inner world is both terrible and strange. In the depths there are monsters as well as kings, and there one cannot go alone.

In our Western society we are conditioned to look for help from outside ourselves. Thus we overlook the fact that the greatest help and healing comes from within. For within us, in the unconscious, are the great archetypal figures of wisdom, the wise old man and the wise old woman. It is they who understand the dynamics of the psyche. It is their work, indeed their most important function, to guide the seeker through the maze of the inner world. Therefore, the Sufi Teacher will always point to the inner Teacher, to the real guide who knows the destiny of the soul. In the dream in which the woman suddenly found herself giving birth there was no doctor or midwife present, 'only a woman who had already had children'. But she was all that was needed, for within us there is the knowledge and understanding of how to give birth to the Self. All we have to do is learn to listen, to allow these unconscious figures to guide us Home.

In this dream the serpent, which inhabited and was contained in the pool, or psyche of the swami, was his friend 'because he had accepted it'. One of the simplest and most fundamental principles of the *opus* is that through being

accepted, 'negative' aspects of the unconscious are transformed and integrated. And in this process love is the
transformative agent. In the words of Christ, 'love thy
neighbour as thyself', for it is by loving what one finds
within oneself that darkness becomes light. Then, rather than
the different aspects of the psyche being in chaotic opposition
to each other, and struggling, fighting for dominance, an
integration takes place. Slowly the aspects of the psyche
become ordered, and a dynamic evolves in which the opposites have their place and are in harmony with each other.
This state of inner harmony in which everything is included
is often portrayed in dreams or art as a mandala, which Jung
discovered to be a recurring symbol for psychological wholeness, or the Self. A mandala images an inner dynamic in
which the many different elements which form the psychological structure of a human being, function in unison. Each
element has its own place and fulfils its true purpose. The
human being becomes like an orchestra in which each
instrument is played in relation to the whole. Then the
profound symphony of the soul can be heard, which in itself
is like one note in the symphony of life. Thus the individual
lives from the depths of himself in harmony with the whole
unfolding pattern of life. This is what Lao Tsu called 'Being
in the Tao', and it is achieved through the simple and yet
infinitely difficult act of loving oneself.

Children need to be loved for themselves, to be loved not
just when they are well-behaved, but at all times. This is the
love the mother can give her child, and it will provide the
growing child with the deepest security. In a similar way,
we need to love ourselves. This is not a selfish love, but in
fact selfless, because it goes beyond the ego. For the ego there
is always good and bad, what is accepted and what is
rejected. Unconditional love belongs to the Self: it mirrors
the way He loves us. He loves us in the wholeness of our
being, in which our 'good' and 'bad' qualities stand equal.
How can He not love all parts of us, when everything is none
other than Himself? Moreover, the Sufi says that He made
us the way He wanted. If He wanted us perfect, He would
have made us perfect. It is only our arrogance and our
ignorance that makes us say we should be other than what

we are. If we are to love Him, we must love the way He
made us.

This quality of acceptance is reflected in a Sufi group, and
people often feel it from the moment they first come. For
many, it is the first time in their life when they feel accepted
for themselves. Nothing is asked, no demands are made, for
the only 'qualification' on the Path is a desire for the Truth.
In the group there is neither hierarchy nor competition. We
are all just 'sinners trying to do better', trying to aspire to
that in us which is Divine, each making our own lonely
journey towards the Truth. 'Swimming in the Infinite
Ocean, who is nearer the shore, and which shore?'

The Teacher does not judge those who come, for once one
has seen the darkness within oneself, then one can no longer
judge another human being. And what right has one to judge
anyway when all is a part of Him? When all is as He wills it
to be? Those who are suited to this Path will remain, while
others will slowly drift away, for the Way of the Heart is not
right for everyone. Some, for example, need a more struc-
tured system. However, all those who are serious seekers are
welcome, and some remain for a month, some for a year,
and some stay for ever.

To be accepted within a group makes it much easier for
one to accept oneself. This is a simple matter of reflection:
the outer environment reflects upon the inner process. But,
to accept oneself does not mean to stop working upon oneself
and becoming psychologically lazy. It does not mean that
one says, 'Well, that's the way I am made, so there is nothing
I can do about it.' One needs to become very self-aware, and
in particular attentive to one's shadow and the desires of the
ego. Great discrimination is needed in order to know when
the shadow is trying to blind one. For example, in India the
idea of karma often makes people blind to the needs of
others. Why should you help someone who is in trouble,
when it is their karma, their fate? But, as Lord Buddha said,
'How do you know that it is not your karma to help them?'

Discrimination is one of the greatest yogic virtues. One
must discriminate in the outside world, to know whom to
help, and how best to help. Similarly, one must learn to
discriminate within. For example, one has to discriminate
between what is a real inner need, a part of oneself that it is

important to express, and what is a desire. It can be psychologically damaging to repress a need, whether this means to have time for personal creativity, or even to go on holiday, but a desire belongs to the ego, from which one is struggling to be free. According to Buddha's teachings, at the root of all suffering is a desire, yet to deny an inner need can also cause suffering. Often the desires of the ego deafen us to the real inner needs of the soul. Then, when the need demands to be heard, it can cause an accident or make us ill, and we are forced to withdraw from the bustle of life, and have time and space to listen within. One friend had a deep need to write a book, but there seemed no space in his life. Then he suddenly caught a 'mysterious illness' which no doctor was able to diagnose. All he found that he could do was to write. He had no energy for anything else. He only wished that he had listened more closely to his dreams and inner promptings. Jung noted that the psyche gives hints; if these are not listened to, it hits. And the unconscious can be drastic in its methods.

To learn to accept oneself is very hard inner work. One must be like a cat at a mousehole, infinitely relaxed and patient, but infinitely attentive. However, this dream of the serpent and the swami offers a spiritual perspective on this process. The dreamer encounters this serpent through being 'merged' with the Teacher figure. 'Merging with the Teacher', *Fana fi'l-Shaikh*, is central to the Sufi Path. It is through first merging with the Teacher, 'a complete self-annihilation in the Master',[2] that the disciple merges with the Prophet, not as man but as Essence, *Fanā fi'l-Rasūl*, and then finally merges with God, *Fanā f'illāh*. In this dream the dreamer is not fully merged, because unlike the swami, he 'was quite frightened', but this important process has begun.

Furthermore, the serpent didn't kill the swami 'because he was surrendered to it', and this gives an insight into the spiritual implications of surrender. For if one is fully surrendered one has already died, and therefore cannot be killed:

When you die of surrender, only then you will live forever,
If you are put to death through surrender,
There is no such thing as death for you,
For you have died already.[3]

Thus the Way of the Sufi, who seeks to 'die before death', is to learn to surrender, to learn to fully accept whatever is given, given by the Teacher, given by life, which is the greatest Guru, given by God – and to surrender to the serpent is to surrender to the primal energy of life.

THE MYSTERY OF LOVE

At the very core of the alchemical *opus* lies the mystery of love. It is love that digests the inner darkness, and it is love that makes one stand naked before the Beloved:

> Nothing is possible without love, not even the process of alchemy, for love puts one in a mood to risk everything and not to withhold important elements.[4]

And the final stage of the *opus* is the *coniunctio*, the union of opposites which is also an embrace of lovers. The following dream, which reads like a fairy tale, images the ecstasy of this union, and has many other important archetypal elements which reflect different aspects of the *coniunctio*:

> I was in a garden party at a palace. It was a very sunny day. I met a prince . . . he came to me and it was as if I knew him. He was very handsome and aristocratic, yet gentle and tender at the same time. He invited me into the palace. I followed him and he looked for a place where we could be together. He found a little corner of a very big room. Even though people were coming through, they didn't disturb us. It was a very private corner. He took off his white cape and set it down on the floor and extended his hand to me to sit with him on the cape. I undressed myself and went to him completely naked. We held each other and had an intense encounter of unity and love. It was an ecstatic union, where we became one.
> Then I found myself walking through the palace. When I crossed one of the big rooms I stopped suddenly because I saw my image reflected in a mirror. I was surprised to see how different I looked. I was wearing a shiny black evening dress and I was pregnant. I knew it was me, but somehow I couldn't see my face. I kept walking through the palace to leave, until I came to a woman sitting in an armchair, staring at me and laughing . . . as if she knew I had a secret. I laughed with her and kept

going, because there was an old man waiting for me in the doorway. He was very familiar to me . . . as if I knew him very well. We embraced . . . and when I separated from his arms I noticed how much his face was changing. He gave me an envelope. He told me I should go back into the palace and inside the envelope was my pass to get in. I took the envelope and went back to talk to the woman. We embraced and started giggling and I knew she knew my secret. So I decided to talk to her about it. I told her I was very much in love with the prince and I was very happy. I left her and went back towards the door. I opened the envelope and inside was a white card with a gold symbol and four gold letters – in a strange calligraphy I couldn't make out.

The dream begins in a garden party at a palace, and while the garden is a Sufi symbol for the world of the soul,[5] the palace, home of the king and queen, symbolises the Self. In this garden of the heart there is a party at which the sun shines, and the meaning of this party unfolds in the course of the dream. For although a dream is often experienced as a sequence of events, the unconscious is neither a temporal nor a sequential reality, and one dream-image or event may contain and mirror other aspects of the dream, offering different amplifications of the same psychic happening. Thus, while the dreamer meets her prince at a party, so their meeting and the union that follows are aspects of the same joyous celebration.

The prince is the dreamer's animus, and therefore 'it was as if I knew him', reflecting the romantic misunderstanding whereby newly met lovers think that they have always known each other, when they are only experiencing the projection of their own animus or anima. However, the animus, like the anima, has different aspects; and the prince, as son of the king, images the aspect of the animus that is closest to the Higher Self. Thus in meeting the prince, the dreamer is meeting the divine aspect of her masculine self, and the purity of this figure is symbolised by the white cape which he gallantly puts on the floor for her to sit on.

The dreamer undresses and goes to her prince 'completely naked', for one can only approach such a union as one's own naked self, unadorned, nothing can be withheld, nothing hidden. The dreamer then describes making love with the prince as 'an intense encounter of unity and love . . . an ecstatic union, where we became one'. As in the dream of the 'Navel of God' this inner union is the alchemical *coniunctio*, in which the sexual partners symbolise the opposites that are united within the psyche. This image of the *coniunctio* as a love affair expresses what for the Sufi is a fundamental truth, that the essence of the *opus* is love; that love is the cause and the means and the outcome. It is the longing for Wholeness, the call of the Beloved, that begins the quest; and love is the fire that burns away the dross, purifying the psyche, pushing the seeker ever onwards; and finally there is the ecstatic union of lovers, as the part returns to the Whole. The Sufi sees nothing in the world but the lover and the Beloved, their separation and their union; and as much as separation is fraught with pain, so is union an experience of bliss, of which the bliss of sexual intercourse is the nearest physical equivalent. Love is the very substance of the Self, and the union with the Self is a lover's meeting.

After making love with the prince the dreamer wanders through the palace, where she sees herself reflected in a mirror: 'I was surprised to see how different I looked. I was wearing a shiny black evening dress and I was pregnant. I knew it was me but somehow I couldn't see my face.' The ecstatic encounter has changed her, for she has experienced the primal unity of the Self, she has touched the hem of the garment of God and now she is pregnant. From this union a child will be born, a child that can be none other than her own divine Self. 'It takes time to make a soul pregnant with God',[6] and for the Sufi this conception is one of the central mysteries of the Path, which our dreamer carries as a 'secret' within her. She also sees herself wearing a black evening dress, and black symbolises the Nothingness, the Void. It is the Emptiness which is also the Fullness of God. Moreover, for the Self to be born one must become nothing, what the Sufi refers to as *fanā*, a state of annihilation. Yet in the mirror the dreamer couldn't see her own face, which suggests that she is not yet fully conscious of the inner change that has happened to her.

Walking through the palace the dreamer came upon a woman 'laughing at me . . . as if she knew I had a secret'.

This woman could represent her shadow, which, belonging to the unconscious, knows her innermost secrets, even those hidden from consciousness. However, at this stage the dreamer does not stay with her 'because there was an old man waiting for me in the doorway'. This is the wise old man, a personification of the Self, and just as the dreamer knew the prince, so she knows the old man who is the deepest part of herself, 'He was very familiar to me . . . as if I knew him very well.' They 'embraced', for her love for the prince is also her love for the old man, and the child within her womb is her closeness to both. In this dream many aspects of the *coniunctio* are reflected, and the lover and the child and the old man are one.

When she separated from the old man the dreamer 'noticed how much his face was changing'. This image describes a profound psychological fact: through a fully felt meeting with an archetype, not only is individual consciousness changed, but so is the archetype itself. The union of love between the lesser and the greater dramatically alters the structure of the psyche, it changes 'the face of the soul'. The divine wisdom personified by the old man is no longer locked in the depths, but now has a direct relationship to consciousness: the dreamer's child is also the old man's child.

The old man gives the dreamer an envelope in which is her pass to enter the palace. In fact her relationship with the old man – their embrace – is her passport to the palace of the Self. But in that the wise old man holds the key of the heart, this symbolic key can be given into the hands of the dreamer, who has thus gained freedom of access into the very core of her own being. However, before the dreamer opens this envelope she 'went back to talk to the woman' and told her of the secret of her love for the prince. If this woman is a shadow figure then this meeting images the important inclusion of the shadow in the transformation of the dreamer. We know from *Sleeping Beauty* the danger of excluding the shadow, for it was the uninvited evil fairy who laid the curse on the new-born princess. But in the story of this dream the shadow is also embraced, and the two women giggle together, suggesting a shared feminine intimacy. Thus the animus, the old man and the shadow are each embraced, and together with the figure of the dreamer they make up the *quaternio*. As in the 'Navel of God' dream which began with the image of the *quaternio*, the *coniunctio* is associated with psychological wholeness.

Finally the dreamer opens the envelope that contains her pass to the palace, and there on a white card is 'a gold symbol and four gold letters', again imaging the *quaternio*. The whiteness of the card suggests purification, echoing the cloak of the prince and the 'blank white sheet' in the dream in which silver dust was moulded into bowls. But on this white card the symbol and the letters are in gold for they are the markings of the Self, which are written 'in strange calligraphy I couldn't make out'. The dreamer has only just entered this inner sanctum of the soul, and she has yet to understand the language of the Self, which is so very different to that of the ego. Towards the very end of his life Jung hinted at this difficulty, and how far from our ordinary understanding lies the mystery of the Self:

> Somewhere there was once a Flower, a Stone, a Crystal, a Queen, a King, a Palace, a Lover and his Beloved, and this was long ago, on an Island somewhere in the ocean five thousand years ago . . . Such is Love, the Mystic Flower of the Soul. This is the Centre, the Self . . . Nobody understands what I mean; only a poet could begin to understand.[7]

8

SYMBOLS OF THE SELF

And it is in fact the paradox which is the highest thing
in the gods' cures (Aristides).

Alchemy is a fundamentally a process of psychological
transformation, whose aim is to transform the *prima materia*,
the undifferentiated contents of the psyche, into the philosopher's stone, the *lapis*, the alchemical symbol for the Self.
Yet, as I have mentioned, the *lapis* is, paradoxically, both the
beginning and the end of the *opus*, as is expressed in the
alchemical idea that 'one must start with a bit of the
philosopher's stone if one is to find it'.[1] In psychological
terms this refers to the fact that it is the Self which individu-
ates itself:

> As the process deepens one realizes more and more that insights
> come by grace and that development occurs not by the will of
> the ego but by the urge to development from the Self.[2]

It is not the ego that makes the journey, nor does it know
the way. The Sufi says 'there exists within the heart of man
a mysterious substance that is both the pilgrim and the Path'.
It is man's immortal Self, the spark within the heart, that
knows the Way Home:

> No one by himself
> can find the Path to Him
> Whoever goes to His street
> goes with His feet.[3]

From a psychological perspective, how much the ego of
the individual ultimately determines the actual dynamic of
the individuation process is unsure. The ego can co-operate,

responding to the guidance offered by the Higher Self in the form of intuitions, dreams and hints. Then the conscious and unconscious work together in harmony. In fact if the individual does not respond to the hints offered by the unconscious, the Self has the ability to attract external situations that force the individual to listen. In the previous chapter I mentioned how the unconscious can cause an illness or an accident. One just 'happens' not to notice a red light . . .

Individuation is a powerful process, channelling energies from the depths of the unconscious. It is particularly important that the individual surrenders to this process, and does not hinder it with unnecessary resistance. This is reflected in the value the Sufi attaches to surrender, for it is the surrender of the ego to the higher Self, that both focuses the individual on the Self, and allows the *opus* to proceed with minimum interference from the ego. Furthermore, it is the role of the Teacher to point the disciple continually in this direction, to remind him of what is really important, as the following dream images:

> A woman has twins which die and this upsets me very much, and yet when I tell this to the Teacher, the Teacher isn't very concerned. When I go to the Teacher's flat I return some food which I had taken from there, but again this doesn't interest her very much. Instead she takes a dark stone from her pocket which glows bright and pulses with light and she says I should take this stone out from time to time and look at it.

In this dream, the dark stone 'which glows bright and pulses with light' is undoubtedly the philosopher's stone, to which the dreamer has access, as the Teacher tells her to 'take this stone out from time to time and look at it'. The philosopher's stone is always in our possession, it is only that it has been forgotten and needs to be uncovered. This dream also makes a valuable distinction between a spiritual and a solely psychological perspective. The 'twins which die' and the 'food which I had taken from her flat' would appear to image psychological disturbances within the dreamer, and yet the Teacher is not interested, but rather turns the attention of the dreamer towards the stone. For the true purpose of the seeker is not to resolve all the problems of the psyche, but rather to realise the Self. From the beginning the Sufi should focus on the goal, the lover long only for the Beloved.

This distinction between the spiritual and the psychological is imaged in another dream from someone in the group who had just begun a Jungian analysis. In this dream the dreamer entered the courtyard of a house where she found a mandala painted on the ground. All around the courtyard were the different rooms of the house in which could be seen various furniture and other things. Discussing this dream within the group it was suggested that the rooms with their different scenes represented the psychological material to be explored and integrated with the help of the analyst, while the mandala imaged the spiritual direction central to her life. It is very significant that the dreamer first discovered the mandala, and then from this central point saw the many rooms around the courtyard. Thus the Self is imaged as consciously forming the central point of reference for all the work to be done in the 'house' of her psyche. Furthermore, while mandala symbolism usually only reveals itself in the course of analysis, pointing towards a hitherto unrealised potential for psychological wholeness, this mandala appeared at the very *beginning* of her analysis. Because the seeker begins with the conscious direction of a desire for the *unio mystica*, the ultimate experience of wholeness, so the symbols of the Self are often evoked at the beginning of the *opus*.

THE JOURNEY INTO DARKNESS

The swan is another symbol for the Self, reflecting its royal associations, and the fact that the swan mates for life. In the following dream of a woman in her early twenties, the symbol of the swan suggests the beginning of spiritual life and the psychological work that this involves:

> I am at a party but I leave because I find it too noisy. I walk down to the beach, and there I see a swan swimming towards the setting sun. I become the swan.

The party which the dreamer finds too noisy is that of a worldly life with its emphasis on sensual pleasure. Rather than being deafened by the noise of this world, the dreamer leaves the party for the quiet of the beach. How often does spiritual life begin with a need for solitude, a need to withdraw into oneself? For it is only when one is alone with oneself that a new direction, a new depth of meaning, can emerge from within. The beach is the symbolic inner place where the waters of the unconscious meet the dry land of consciousness; and there, from out of the unconscious comes the image of a swan. In her act of leaving the party the dreamer has evoked from the depths of her unconscious this symbol of the Self, with which she identifies, 'I become the swan.' Thus she begins her spiritual journey, leaving the shores of this world for the infinite ocean.

But why in this dream is the swan swimming towards the setting sun? Surely this departure should be towards the rising sun, symbolising the dawn of a new consciousness? The answer is given in an alchemical text quoted by Jung:

'Know,' says Ripley, 'that your beginning should be made towards sunset, and that from there you should turn towards midnight, when the lights cease altogether to shine, and you should remain ninety nights in the dark fire of purgatory without light. Then turn your course towards the east, and you will pass through many different colours.'[4]

And to this Jung comments: 'The alchemical work starts with the descent into darkness (*nigredo*), i.e. the unconscious.' Thus, symbolised as 'a swan swimming towards the setting sun', the dreamer is embarking on the great journey into the depths of the unconscious. Furthermore, as in the dream of the mandala in the courtyard, her psychological work commences with an identification with the Self. She begins with the *lapis*. It is the higher Self of the dreamer that will take her on this journey beyond the horizon.

For those not on a spiritual path, their psychological *opus* will be consciously directed towards living in a more balanced and integrated manner, and indeed Jung stressed the importance of living 'in *this* world, and *this* life'. Naqshbandi Sufism does not dismiss this world, as already mentioned it is neither a monastic nor ascetic Path. The Sufi lives in the world, and may bring up a family, be a craftsman or businessman, yet his primary orientation is towards another reality, and ultimately 'this world becomes nothing, non existent'. And so, although the psychological material may reflect problems about living in this world, the whole *opus* is focused on the beyond. Thus, in the previous dream the woman's journey (both spiritual and psychological) points away from the party of life and the shores of this world.

The Self is both the beginning and the end of the spiritual quest, a quest which takes the seeker far from the security of the known world. And yet the birth of the Self is the most natural process. The Self is often imaged by a baby or child. I have looked at two dreams which use the symbolism of the dreamer giving birth to a child. In the first the dreamer was a man 'watching his own birth.'[5] He was 'both the father and the child', and the divine nature of the child was reflected in a feeling of 'great peace' and the image of 'flames on the bed', flames which were a 'holy fire' because they did not burn and could not be put out. In the other dream, the dreamer was a woman who saw the head of her child beginning to come out, and knew that the birth 'was going to be very painful, might even rip me apart'.[6] The birth of the Self is a painful process, the seeker is consumed by the sacred fire of his own longing which burns in the heart and is unquenchable. The following dream also alludes to this divine birth, and points to its 'dark side'. The central quality of this dream is a feeling of fear:

> There was a tremendous feeling of fear in this dream. Three old men got into my flat under false pretenses (saying that they were delivering a package) or they actually broke in. They were shabbily dressed and looked like hobos. They were small and they dropped off a package and then walked down the hallway looking in all the rooms. I was absolutely petrified and unable to speak. I tried to yell but nothing came out. I broke a glass, thinking I could use it as a weapon, and walked down the hall. They left and I rang the police so that they could be caught. I then opened the package that the old men had left behind, and while I was talking to the police, I saw that the package was in fact for me. There was a letter, but I didn't look at it . . . I was

curious but still very frightened and suspicious to see what was inside. The first thing I saw was flowers. Then there were three gifts, beautifully wrapped in lovely paper. I opened one, but I think it had even lovelier wrapping paper inside. I was still frightened about the old men. The dream ended before I could see what the gifts were or who wrote the note.

The three old men leaving gifts echo three other men who brought gifts, gifts for a child born in a manger. The old men who looked like hobos are the Magi, and their gifts point towards the birth of the Self. In fact there is a suggestion that the Magi who came to honour the birth of Christ were early Sufis. They were the *Sophos*, the wise men from the East. There is a legend such men also came to Socrates, shortly before his death, to warn him of the danger he was in, and also visited Plato. It was said that these wise men used to move their lips in silent prayer, a custom which was not known to the Greeks. People would see them moving their lips without talking, and when asked, the *Sophos* said that they were praying. This is the silent *dhikr*, the remembrance of God, practised by the Sufis.

But why were these three men in the dream dressed like hobos rather than kings, and why was the dreamer so frightened? As I have mentioned Sufis are known as 'Travellers' or 'Wayfarers on the Mystical Path', following the saying of the Prophet 'Be in this world as if you are a traveller, a passer-by, with your clothes and shoes full of dust.' Sufis are like tramps, not in the sense that they wear old clothes, but in the sense that in this world they have no real home, they do not belong here. Sufis belong somewhere else. They belong to their Beloved. In the great Eastern love story of Layla and Majnun, Majnun became so lost in his love for Layla that he became mad, and lived in the desert, forgetting everything but the name of his Beloved. His father, who was a wealthy man, was in total despair, because he wanted to leave all his money to Majnun, but all Majnun could say was

I have not only lost you; I no longer know myself. Who am I? I keep turning upon myself, asking 'What is your name? Are you

in love? With whom? Or are you loved? By whom . . .' A flame
burns in my heart, a flame beyond measure, which has turned
my being to ashes. Do I still know where I live? Do I still taste
what I eat? I am lost in my own wilderness! I have become a
savage with wild beasts as my companions. Do not try to bring
me back to the world of humans! Believe me, I am a stranger
to them. One must not keep a melon in the garden once it has
been poisoned by a fly, lest it infect the others. I am drawn
towards death – death is within me. If only you could forget that
you ever had a son! If only you could erase me from the book
of those born into the world. If only you could bury me here
and think: Some fool, some drunken madman . . . What was to
be expected of him?[7]

Thus it is not surprising that the dreamer is frightened by
the old men, for if one seriously embarks on the Path of
Love, one becomes, like Majnun, lost to this world. Maybe
it does not happen so dramatically, but it happens. In fact the
dreamer was already facing this crisis, in that she was in her
mid-thirties, having given up a successful career in order to
be with her Teacher; and her mother was worried about her
because she didn't have a proper job, or a house, or a
husband, or children.

In the eyes of the world the Sufi is mad. We are in love
with an invisible Beloved! We want the Nothingness! We
don't care about job, career, position, salary! All that matters
is the greatest adventure, the Path to the Infinite. And once
you seriously begin, you can't go back. For there is nowhere
to go back to. The world no longer exists as it used to. It no
longer makes sense. And you have lost your old friends
anyway, for they gave up with you. Here is the value of a
spiritual group, to be in the company of other Wayfarers
who have the same values. The Sufi group is like a sacred
space in this world, a 'home from home'. This is why the
Sufis attach so much importance in just 'being together'. At
our group meetings we meditate and discuss dreams, but we
also drink tea and gossip, are just 'together'. On your own,
surrounded by people who see life in a *totally* different way,
it is *very difficult*. It is much easier when one is in the company
of friends who are also making this impossible journey, who

talk the same language, and have the same 'madness'. A
cartoon depicts a mystic walking past a madman who is tied
up in a straight-jacket. The madman says to the mystic,
'How come you are walking around free, while I am tied up
like this?' The mystic replies, 'I knew who to talk to and you
did not.'

The importance of the Teacher is that he is one who has
been There and knows the Way. The Teacher knows the
value of what you are looking for, knows that it is worth
paying the very highest price. And yet a Teacher does not
force the seeker to give up the world, he just shows you
something much more beautiful:

> A Yogi was telling his beads by the Ganges when a Brahmin in
> rags came to him and said, 'Help me, I am poor!'
> 'My alms-bowl is all that is my own,' said the Yogi. 'I have
> given away everything I had.'
> 'But my lord Shiva came to me in my dreams,' said the
> Brahmin, 'and counselled me to come to you.'
> The Yogi suddenly remembered he had picked up a stone
> without price among the pebbles on the river-bank, and thinking
> that someone might need it hid it in the sands.
> He pointed out the spot to the Brahmin, who wondering dug
> up the stone.
> The Brahmin sat on the earth and mused alone till the sun
> went down behind the trees, and cowherds went home with
> their cattle. Then he rose and came slowly to the Yogi and said,
> 'Master, give me the least fraction of the wealth that disdains all
> the wealth of the world.'
> And he threw the precious stone into the water.[8]

In order to awaken to the Reality of the inner world, one
must turn away from the glittering dance of Maya. This
process is described in a man's dream, in which there is again
the central image of a swan:

> A statue of a swan comes to life and starts to blind my eyes.

The swan, as a symbol of the Self, begins to blind the
dreamer to the things of this world, for it is only when one's
eyes are blind to this world of illusion that one's single inner
eye, 'the eye of the heart', can open to the world of Reality.
In the words of Lao Tsu:

Without looking through the window, you may see the ways
of heaven.
The farther you go, the less you know.⁹

Thus it is the function of the higher Self to take the seeker's
attention away from this world, to make this world meaningless, before it can reveal a world that is not Maya.

It is significant to note that this dream starts with the swan
as a statue coming to life. This relates to the fact that one
begins spiritual life with the dim knowledge that one has a
transcendent centre of consciousness, but because one has
little or no conscious experience of it, one creates a psychological image of the Self, which then awakens and has a life
of its own. Creating an image of the Self is a necessary first
step: indeed it is said that first you create an image of God
and then God creates you; He then becomes alive within you
and transforms you. For without this primary image of the
Self, or God, there is no space in the psyche for this higher
reality to manifest. Of course the experience of this reality,
the swan coming to life, will be totally different to any
preconceived image, but the image forms an important
conscious direction for the seeker. In fact, this image will act
as a nodal point in the psyche which helps to focus both
consciousness and the unconscious towards the Self.

From a Jungian perspective this image of the Self acts as
the 'transcendent function'. The 'transcendent function' is
Jung's term for a function which facilitates a transition from
one psychological attitude or condition to another. It bridges
'the gulf between CONSCIOUSNESS and the UNCONSCIOUS'.¹⁰
Thus the conscious creation of an idea or image of the Self
forms a bridge that allows the Self and its accompanying
psychological/spiritual condition to arise out of the unconscious and become manifest.

The whole approach to a spiritual quest often has the same
dynamic. At the beginning, the seeker forms some idea of
what spiritual life is and to what he is aspiring. This idea may
be formed from books or assimilated from various spiritual
traditions, and it is a conscious direction which, combined
with an inner discontent, longing or aspiration, takes the
seeker on to a spiritual path. However once the seeker pro-
gresses on the Path, so any such preconceptions will go, for

>The Tao that can be told is not the Tao.
>The name that can be named is not the name.[11]

Any true spiritual path will take one beyond the mind and its concepts, and so although a conscious direction and idea about spiritual life is helpful at the beginning, forming a focus for aspiration, it will dissolve as the real Path comes to life within the seeker. Then, rather than any external or conceptualised image, the Path becomes a living and dynamic reality within the psyche – the Way and the pilgrim become one.

Thus the seeker may begin with a conscious conception about the Path, which allows the real Path to infuse itself into the unconscious and be slowly digested. Yet the following dream suggests that there comes a time when this unconscious process needs to become conscious, and interestingly the dreamer is slightly reticent for this to happen:

>I am invited to a meal. There are lots of beautifully cooked different foods, but there are also some books which I need to eat. I am slightly reticent about eating these books, but I eat some food, including a deliciously grilled fish. I then start to eat a book, with a green cover and pictures of castles. I find that it tastes delicious. I embrace the woman friend who invited me to the meal and there is a feeling of great love.

The Path offers much nourishment, of which the seeker is invited to partake; yet beside the cooked foods there are also books which she needs to eat. Books suggest conscious knowledge, and the dreamer would rather be nourished by the unconscious, 'a deliciously grilled fish', than by these books. But she does 'start to eat a book' one with 'a green cover'. Green is a very auspicious colour, it is the colour of growth and becoming; and, according to Sufism, it is also the colour of the realisation of God. There is a very important Sufi figure called 'Khiḍr', or the 'Green One' who is associated with the direct revelation of the divine world. In the dreamer's book are 'pictures of castles' and castles, according to Jung, are symbols of the Self.[12] This implies that the dreamer needs to complement the unconscious nourishment offered by the Path with some conscious understanding of what is meant by the Self.

The book that the dreamer needs to eat does not imply that she needs to study texts, because everything in the dream is within her. The dream would rather suggest that she needs to make conscious what it means to live in relationship with her higher Self. Whether her reticence, 'I am slightly reticent about eating these books', merely reflects the unusual image of having to eat books, or is caused by a certain resistance to becoming conscious in this manner, would only be known by the dreamer. However, it is often the case that an inner drive towards consciousness is met with a certain resistance. But when the dreamer actually eats this book she finds that it 'tastes delicious'; a conscious understanding of what is embodied in the Self must be one of the most delicious foods man can taste.

Finally, the dreamer 'embraces the woman friend who invited me to the meal'. Whether this woman is an aspect of the higher Self, a helpful part of her personality, or an aspect of the shadow is unsure; though it is worth remembering that the shadow is not always unhelpful, and at times pushes us to become more conscious. But what is important is that at the end of the dream there is 'a feeling of great love', for love is the essence of the Sufi Path, and the journey towards the Self is a lover's return to the arms of the Beloved, in whose embrace all the aspects of the psyche are contained in oneness and 'great love'.

THE CITY OF THE SELF

Just as within the dreamer's green book are the pictures of castles, so the quest for psychological wholeness is contained within a greater quest. In this chapter I have suggested that the Sufi focuses on the beyond, and that in so doing he does not, as Jung might imply, reject the need for psychological integration; but rather this integration takes place through the commitment to a spiritual goal. This process is beautifully illustrated in the following dream:

I go with my wife to the races and bet on two horses, but instead of a ticket, I got a piece of wood carved with the names of the horses. I then left the race-course and drove off, but then came to another race-course and went to find what had happened at the races, where I found that our horses had won. I was to receive £40,000. I then remembered that the name of one of the horses was 'al-Haqq' ('The Truth' in Arabic).

The horses can represent either the emotional energy, or the life energy, libido, of the dreamer. Four, according to Jung, is the number of wholeness. Therefore, the winnings of £40,000 image integration and the substantial value or energy (for money often symbolises energy) that this gives to the dreamer. But of course the significance of the dream rests in the name of the horse, al-Haqq; for it was by betting on the Truth that the process of integration occurred. The focus of the dreamer was not on the psychological activity of integrating his emotional energy or libido, and indeed when discussing the dream he mentioned that he was surprised both by winning and by the amount won. But the dream makes an important statement about the psychological dynamics of this Sufi Path, where the seeker's longing for spiritual truth works as an alchemical catalyst, activating the psyche's drive towards wholeness, whether imaged as a symbol of the Self or the simple number four.

However, it is important to remember that these symbols of the Self not only image psychological wholeness, but, like all archetypal images, also translate into consciousness the reality of another dimension. Yet, while all other archetypal images describe the '*mundus imaginalis*', the imaginal world of the collective unconscious, the symbols of the Self point to a wholly transcendent dimension that cannot be understood from a psychological perspective. For although the Self can be described as the totality of the psyche, it is in essence a centre of divine consciousness that exists 'outside' the psyche.[13] It is beyond the reach of the mind and can only be truthfully depicted in paradoxes:

> Unmoving, the One is swifter than the mind.
> Speeding ahead, it outruns the gods of the senses.
> Past others running, it goes standing.
> . . .
> It moves. It moves not.
> Far, yet near.

Within all,
Outside all.[14]

Furthermore, the symbols of the Self as experienced in dreams contain the seeds of that transcendent Reality, seeds that can slowly germinate within the human being. And sometimes a dream tries to communicate an experience of the Self, as in the following dream. The dreamer is a man.

> I am with a woman whom I do not know personally, and I make a journey in search of something. We return to the High Street empty-handed, having found nothing.
>
> I go directly to the Teacher's house and enter the room which leads to the Teacher's garden. The Teacher is in the room, standing by the wall at my left and wearing black.
>
> I look into the garden. As I do so the space in which the room, the Teacher and I exist undergoes a transformation, becomes a kind of 'skeletal' space, in the matrix of which another dimension is revealed.
>
> I see a city that appears to be made of light, or permeated with light. Completely integral, the city in the distance is like a great palace, unitary, unfragmented, whole. I see the city from end to end. The light of which it is composed is fascinating but difficult to describe. There are different levels or dimensions of light. 'Dimensions' not in the sense of geometric relations inherent in our experience of physical space and perspective. Rather it is Light-Within-Light, so to speak; something I cannot explain in terms of the logic of perceptions familiar to everyday waking consciousness.

This dream begins with the theme of the search; the dreamer, together with an unknown woman, who is suggestive of the anima, searching for something which they do not find. Just as a previous dreamer left a party for the beach, so empty-handed, this dreamer leaves the High Street and its worldly values and goes directly to the house of the Teacher, for what the dreamer is looking for cannot be found in the market place.

Entering the room which leads to the Teacher's garden, the dreamer sees the Teacher on her left, wearing black. Black is no colour; it represents 'mystical poverty', a state of total annihilation in God:

It has been said that mystical poverty is the wearing of the black raiment in the two universes. This saying expresses the fact that the mystic is so totally absorbed in God that he has no longer any existence of his own, neither inwardly nor outwardly in this world and beyond; he returns to his original essential poverty, and that is poverty in the true sense. It is in this sense, when the state of poverty has become total, that a mystic can say that he is God . . .[15]

Moreover, in the dream it is significant that the Teacher is on the dreamer's left, for as I have mentioned this is a feminine Path that works through the unconscious. The dreamer then looks into the garden, upon which 'the space in which the room, the Teacher and I exist undergoes a transformation'. The garden is a symbolic image for the inner world of the soul, particularly for the Sufi who sees in the beauty and sweet fragrance of the garden the reflection of an Infinite Beauty:

> What is all beauty in the world? The image,
> Like quivering boughs reflected in a stream,
> Of that eternal Orchard which abides
> Unwithered in the hearts of Perfect Men.[16]

In turning his attention away from the outside world towards the inner reality of the heart, the dreamer is shown how the Teacher and her room, are essentially a 'skeletal' space within which another dimension can be revealed. This is a very profound statement about the nature of a Sufi Teacher who, 'totally absorbed in God', is nothing but a space within which the seeker can realise Another Reality. Essentially the Teacher does not exist.

What the dreamer experiences within this 'skeletal' space is a city made of light, which the dreamer sees in its entirety, 'unitary, unfragmented, whole'. Such an image clearly points to the Self, to our own divine nature in which everything has its true place, everything is included. On the level of the Self there is no duality, no sense of separation, only oneness. This 'city' seen in the distance echoes the heavenly city of Jerusalem shown to St John the Divine by an angel:

And he carried me away in the spirit to a great and high

mountain, and he shewed me that great city, the holy Jerusalem, descending out of heaven from God.

Having the glory of God: and her light was like unto a stone most precious, even like a jasper stone, clear as crystal.

[. . .]

And the building of the wall of it was of jasper; and the city was pure gold, like unto clear glass.

And the foundations of the wall of the city were garnished with all manner of precious stones. The first foundation was jasper; the second saphire; the third, a chalcedony; the fourth an emerald;

The fifth, sardonyx; the sixth, sardius; the seventh, chrysolyte; the eighth, beryl; the ninth, topaz; the tenth, a chrysoprasus; the eleventh, a jacinth; the twelfth, an amethyst.

And the twelve gates were twelve pearls; every several gate was of one pearl: and the street of the city was pure gold, as it were transparent glass.

And I saw no temple therein: for the Lord God Almighty and the Lamb are the temple of it.

And the city had no need of the sun, neither of the moon, to shine in it: for the glory of God did lighten it, and the Lamb is the light thereof.[17]

In both the dream and the vision of St John the city of the Self is visible in its entirety, for the dreamer 'an unfrag-mented whole'; for St John a mandala image. Furthermore, each description tries to convey a transparency and lumin-osity: the dreamer's city is 'permeated with light', the heavenly Jerusalem is 'pure gold like unto clear glass' and 'the glory of God did lighten it'. Finally, in both images there is a sense of different 'levels': in the dream there are 'different levels or dimensions of light', and in St John's vision the city has different levels of foundation, seven in all. However, the dreamer insists that these 'dimensions are not in the sense of geometric relations inherent in our everyday experience of physical space and perspective', and St John's city is 'coming down from God out of heaven', and thus its geometric proportions belong to another Reality.

This dream of a city made of light points to the transcen-dent Reality that lies behind the symbols of the Self. This is a dimension totally different to that of 'everyday waking consciousness'; it is a world of 'Light-Within-Light' that cannot be described or explained in terms of our normal perception. This is why it is said, 'Of those who made the journey no news returns'. There are no words to describe the world of Truth. Yet the similarity of this dreamer's city with that experienced two thousand years earlier by St John, suggests that this inner Reality has certain definite qualities of wholeness and luminosity, though they can only be hinted at.

For the Sufi, this inner world of light, 'the Throne', lies behind the veil of the sensible world, and is reached through the heart. And within the heart is the light of the Self, the 'man of light', which, when the heart opens, merges with its source, the Divine Light of God:

> When this veil [the veil of the sensible world] is rent and a door to the Throne opens in the heart, like springs towards like. Light rises towards light and light comes down upon light, *'and it is light upon light'* (*Koran* 24:35).[18]

Spiritual life is the simple process of unlocking the door in the heart. When this door is open then His Light fills your life, and everything you experience becomes permeated with Him. His Light, which is none other than the Light of your own Divine Self, shines in your face.

The symbols of the unconscious are like keys which can open the door between the world of the senses and the world of light, the inner world of the soul. To conclude this chapter I would like to tell a dream that, together with the dreamer's own comments, describes the transformative effect that a symbol of the Self can have within the psyche. A symbol of the Self may first cause discomfort, because, like all symbols of the unconscious, it places an 'ethical responsibility' upon the individual, who must understand and integrate it into his life, as far as is possible. Furthermore, as in the dream of the statue of the swan blinding the dreamer's eyes, a symbol of the Self slowly turns the psyche and the focus of consciousness away from the world of the senses, and this can be a painful process. But finally, as images of both the wholeness of the psyche and our divine nature, these symbols imprint themselves within the human being, reconnecting individual consciousness with the Self. Thus they open a door through which the individual can pass on his journey from a world of illusion to the world of Reality. And for the Sufi, this whole process always takes place under the guidance of the Teacher:

> I dreamt that I was taken to a large room where there were a number of people, male and female. At one end sat a spiritual Teacher, who instructed us to go to the opposite side of the room where there was a large table covered with objects. All these objects were to be worn on the physical body, and would cause considerable discomfort, even pain. I remember seeing a hair shirt, and something to be worn around the head and fastened tightly. I chose a round pebble, to be placed in the shoe and worn all the time. I took the pebble and placed it in the shoe, and walked towards the door. As I was leaving the Teacher shouted after me, 'It is possible to wear it, without it hurting too much.'

> I awoke from this dream feeling very 'high', full of lightness and ecstasy. To ground myself somewhat I went for a walk, and all the time the symbology of the pebble haunted me like this:

> The pebble is a part of the stone, the symbol of the Self.
> It will make an imprint on my foot – a merging with the Beloved.
> The foot is a replica of the whole body, which will become impregnated with the Self.
> Ultimately there will be a complete merging between the pebble and myself – a Oneness – the circle of the pebble will enclose my heart.

TEACHING DREAMS

He who walks towards Me, I come to him running
(The *Hadith*)

Some dreams, rather than offering psychological guidance, give specific spiritual teaching, and are therefore known as 'teaching dreams'. On occasions this 'teaching' can be very simple and direct, as in the following dream:

> The Teacher is with us in a big party where we all have to sing children's songs. One woman wants to sing a song called 'Smile'. The song was simply: 'Smile, smile, smile, smile etc.' The Teacher stops her and says:
> 'We have no time for songs like that. We have time for songs of endurance and uncertainty and doubt which lead to perseverance.'
> The Woman is upset. The Teacher lovingly asks her:
> 'Would you like to write a dissertation on endurance and uncertainty and doubt?'
> The woman says yes and leaves to do her work.

This dream needs little interpretation, except to add a sentence another member of the group heard in a dream – 'Turned soft by a very hard system'. For although the Naqshbandi System is without outer form or imposed discipline (there is no set time for meditation, no structure of spiritual exercises), it requires great perseverance to endure the intense longing and psychological pressures to which the Wayfarer is subjected. On this Path there is a long period in which the road is very stony, and only those who have the will to endure can pass this stage. The world becomes empty and meaningless, friends fall away, and yet the spiritual experiences have not yet begun. When the seeker has had experiences then the Path is to some degree easier, for faith can be supported by the reality of these experiences, and yet often the mind will still doubt and cause difficulties. The grinding down of the personality is a slow and painful process, and on the Path the seeker is pushed to the limit of his endurance and seemingly beyond.

One has to 'just to hold on . . . in spite of everything':

> If you can force your heart and nerve and sinew
> To serve your turn long after they are gone,
> And so hold on when there is nothing in you
> Except the Will which says to them 'Hold on!'[1]

In the Naqshbandi System the difficulties faced by the Wayfarer are primarily psychological: often one's sense of security and identity is taken away; and, confronted only by the darkness of one's own psyche, one is left alone and forlorn. In this state there is nothing one can do but cry out from the depths of one's heart, and only the Great Beloved can help – in the words of Rumi, 'And I will cry to Thee and cry to Thee, and keep crying until the Milk of Thy Kindness boils up.' Thus the Sufi is taken to the point where he sees his only salvation in the arms of his Beloved; and finally, out of the hardness of this System is born the tenderness and softness of a lover's heart which has been melted by the embrace of his Beloved – for, as it is said, a Sufi is one whose heart 'is as soft and as warm as wool'.

However, this whole process of transformation only takes place through the Wayfarer surrendering to the difficulties and hardships of the Path. I have already mentioned the importance of surrender, but in the following teaching dream it is associated with 'growing up':

> A man was lying on a bed crying because he wanted to grow up. One woman present said, 'That means to become self sufficient'.
>
> But a man who was also present said, 'No, it means to surrender.'

This dream contrasts two perspectives on 'growing up', the worldly and the spiritual. In the development of the child, life begins with total dependency on the mother, first within the womb, and then, all being well, as a suckling infant. But as the child grows it should naturally become more and more self-sufficient, until finally it leaves home and makes a life for itself, away from the protection and support of the parents. This pattern can be seen in the development of animals as much as with humans, though many human psychological problems are caused by parents not allowing this process to take place, and, often unconsciously, forcing the child to remain dependent.

What happens during this natural development is that the ego of the child establishes its own individuality, and thus 'growing up' becomes a process of learning to live one's own life separate from both the support and the demands of one's parents. However, being sufficient unto oneself is essentially a perspective on life dominated by the ego, in which nothing is more important than one's own individual self. And although it is vitally important to learn to stand on one's own feet, there can come a time when the ego and its desires become limited, and one seeks for more than the fulfilment of the little self.

Jung felt that the stage of 'ego development' started at puberty with the 'psychic birth' of the individual, and continued until middle life, which begins 'between the thirty-fifth and fortieth year'.[2] During this period the individual is primarily concerned with adapting to the outside world, developing his abilities etc. Then 'in the secret hour of life's midday . . . death is born',[3] and a psychological change takes place. Faced with death, the individual can either cling to the values of the ego, or question them, and begin to look into the beyond.

But now, twenty years after Jung's death, it would seem that many young people are not prepared to wait until middle age to begin their inner quest. Possibly this is because we are now in the death throes of the Piscean era, and are surrounded on all sides by the signs of this decaying civilisation in which the values of the ego are shown to be polluting rather than developing life. At this time the life-cycle of the whole planet profoundly affects the consciousness of many sensitive people, pushing them to search and to question.

For the Sufi, the journey beyond the confines of the ego is the essence of the Path. The ego sees this life and its worldly values as all that exists. How can the ego think otherwise? It only knows this physical plane of existence. Indeed the purpose of the ego is to help the soul to experience this world. The ego belongs to this world of duality, and without an ego we could not function here. But there is a deeper part of ourselves for whom this physical life is but a momentary interlude in a vast unfolding pattern. On the level of the soul this life has a purpose which belongs to aeons and millennia, and is very different to the momentary glimpse afforded by the ego. Spiritual life is learning to listen to this deeper purpose, learning to allow the soul to unfold into our life. Then the immortal part of ourselves can live through us, and the deeper meaning of our life slowly flower.

Spiritual life is a journey Home, it is a journey from the ego back to our immortal Self. But the Self cannot be reached through the mind or by the will of the ego, only through surrender. By surrendering the seeker becomes empty, and into that emptiness the Beloved can enter and reveal Himself. Here is another of the paradoxes of the Path, that it is *effortless*. The Sufi does nothing but surrender, because from a spiritual perspective everything is a gift:

> How can there be an effort with Divine things? They are given, infused . . . Divine things can never be forced, however right, however correct is the attitude of the Shishya. It is given as a gift.[4]

This Path, which demands the utmost effort is at the same time, effortless. The effort is in the waiting, in the endurance, in the longing. The effort is in 'holding on . . . in spite of everything', in spite of the doubts, the difficulties, the states of psychological crisis. But finally, everything is His gift, and it is always more than one could ever even imagine.

Thus through this dream of the man lying on the bed wanting to grow up, the dreamer is told that, from a spiritual perspective, maturity is not being 'self-sufficient' but surrendering. To 'grow up' is to learn to be totally dependent on the guidance and nourishment that comes from within. In this sense it echoes the dream of the 'Navel of God' in which the dreamer is shown a landscape which images this state of the annihilation of the lower self. Furthermore, in both these dreams the dreamer was a woman, and yet a central part was played by an animus figure. In this teaching dream it was a man who was 'lying on a bed crying because he wanted to grow up'. Here the animus images the dreamer's relationship to the outside world, for as much as surrender is a state of inner devotion, so is it reflected in one's attitude to life. In a recent television interview Mother Theresa described what a life of surrender really means:

> Everyday we have to say yes – total surrender. To be where He wants you to be. If He puts you in the street, if everything is taken from you, when you suddenly find yourself in the street, to accept to be in the street at *that* moment. Not to move, not for you to put yourself in the street, but to accept to be put there. This is quite different. To accept if God wants you to be in a palace, well then to accept to be in the palace so long as you are not choosing to be in the palace. This is the difference. This is what makes the difference in total surrender. To accept what He gives and to give whatever He takes with a big smile. This is the surrender to God. To accept to be cut to pieces and yet every bit belonging only to Him. This is the surrender. To accept all the people that come, the work that you happen to do. To *accept*. And to give whatever it takes; it takes your good name, it takes your health, it takes . . . yes, you are free then.

This freedom described by Mother Theresa is the *total* opposite to our Western view of freedom, which is the freedom to do what you want, to fulfil the desires of the ego. But as I have suggested, spiritual values are completely different to those of the ego, and here is another seeming paradox: to be free is to be His slave, to do what He wants you to do. Spiritual freedom is that of absolute surrender, the surrender of the ego to the Divine that is within us; for, however it may appear, such surrender is always to the Higher Self. Furthermore, to learn to surrender is the most difficult thing while you are doing it, and the easiest thing when it is done. Why? Because once one has surrendered to That which is within, the ego has 'died', and then one has no other desire but to do His will – for the Sufi as for the

Christian 'Thy will be done'. Here lies the secret of 'Yogic contentment':

> If His will be done always, whatever happens to me in life is fine. If I suffer and so what? I offer my suffering to Him, to the Beloved. The whole life is changed.[5]

Such an attitude reflects a profound spiritual maturity, in which life, rather than being goal-orientated, becomes a state of being.

THE GUIDED LIFE

That spiritual life is a state of being is imaged by the following dream, in which the Teacher 'moves without moving':

> I saw the Teacher floating face down in the most beautiful crystal clear water with her silver hair streaming behind her, and her arms, which seemed then to become wings, reaching backwards by her side. She seemed to be moving and yet not moving; the water seemed to just float past her, and there were beautiful bubbles, so perfect, all drifting by. It was so wonderful to see.

Here, in the clear water of life, floats the Teacher. Her hair streams behind and the water passes by, and yet she appears to make no effort. This dream has the quality of a spiritual vision, and its crystal-clear water echoes that shown to St John the Divine:

> And he showed me a pure river of water of life, clear as crystal, proceeding out of the throne of God and of the Lamb.[6]

Thus the dreamer is given a spiritual perspective on life that is both beautiful and profound.

At the time of this dream, the dreamer was thinking that she should do something more useful with her life, and the dream provides an answer as clear as the water: spiritual life is a state of being. Sufism is very similar to Zen in that it is learning to sit without sitting, meditate without meditating, go without going. This again may appear paradoxical to the

Western mind, but it simply means that the seeker should allow life to take its natural course, and not 'try to do anything'. For, unless we are following the guidance of the Higher Self, any attempt we may make to 'do something' has its origins in the ego, and is thus not only limited, but is also working against a process that seeks to take us beyond the ego. Within us are the seeds of our own fulfilment, which is not the fulfilment of the ego, but of our very essence. And these seeds will germinate and grow if we allow them, and do not interfere. Thus, in the wisdom of Lao Tsu,

> Less and less is done
> Until non-action is achieved.
> When nothing is done, nothing is left undone.
>
> The world is ruled by letting things take their course.
> It cannot be ruled by interfering.[7]

There is much arrogance in our Western attitude towards progress and achievement, and its results can be seen in the ecological disaster that is the product of mankind 'improving' his life-style. But just as we are becoming aware that mankind is part of a larger ecological pattern, so psychology reveals that ego consciousness is only a small part of an infinitely larger psychic wholeness. Therefore, if man is to allow his complete self to reach fulfilment, rather than just his limited ego, he must put aside his conditioned perception of what is 'useful', and allow a larger pattern to unfold its meaning – a pattern in which all aspects of life are in harmony. In the following story by Chang Tzu, a tree, a symbol of life itself, reveals a spiritual purpose through being totally 'useless':

A master carpenter and his assistant were passing a very great tree, which was venerated by all the people around, and was used as an altar by the spirits of the land. It was so great a tree that an oxen standing behind it might not be seen.

The assistant said to his master, 'What a wonderful tree.' But the master did not agree, 'It is quite useless. A boat made from its wood would sink, a coffin would quickly rot, furniture would fall to pieces, a pillar would be eaten by insects. Its material is good for nothing, hence it has attained so great an age.'

But that night the spirit of the tree came to him in a dream and said, 'You say I am good for nothing. If I had been useful I would long ago have been cut down. If I had been a fruit bearing tree, my branches would have been broken when they knocked down the fruit. Their productive ability makes their lives bitter and they come to a premature end. It is because I am so totally useless that I have grown to so great an age, and so provided an altar for these people to worship and revere the spirits of the land.'

For the Friend of God it is only as His slave that life has any meaning. It is only through being used by Him that one is useful, just as it is only through being empty that one is full. Sufis are workers, 'Servants of the People', and to use the words of Albert Schweitzer, 'we are involved in humanity'. In whatever walk of life destiny places him, whether as a politician, a gardener or an artist, the Sufi serves the purpose of the One who guides him. Moreover, just as 'the pen cannot understand the words that it is writing', neither does the Sufi seek to understand the purpose of his actions, but rather follows in total surrender the promptings of the heart. In fact the Sufi himself does not attempt to help or better any situation, for in so doing he would be viewing the situation from the perspective of the ego, which only has a limited vision, and never sees the whole. This is illustrated by a true story of a western woman in India, who, entering the courtyard of her Guru, saw a dog in a state of great discomfort, foaming at the mouth, tied to a tree by a piece of string. The string was tied so tightly around the neck that it was cutting into the skin and the neck was bleeding. A crowd of children were standing around watching. Feeling sorry for the dog, the woman cut the piece of string with her nail scissors, whereupon the dog promptly bit her, bit one of the children, who was the Guru's daughter, and then ran off down the street. The Guru, aroused by the commotion, came into the courtyard, and seeing what had happened, was furious with the woman because the dog had rabies. The dog had just been tied up, awaiting the arrival of the man who would take him away. The woman went immediately to the hospital to have a series of very painful injections in the stomach, but when she offered to take the Guru's daughter he said it was not necessary. The woman later discovered that the dog had run down the street and bitten a number of people before being shot. Some of these people subsequently died, but when the woman returned from the hospital and again asked about the Guru's daughter, he just said 'She will be alright. I gave her a glass of water.'

The Sufi learns to listen within, and to follow his inner guidance with total faith and obedience. This is what it means to 'lead a Guided Life – guided by that in us which is Eternal'. And in following this inner thread during the course of his daily affairs the Sufi practises 'Solitude in the Crowd': 'outwardly to be with the people, inwardly to be with God'. Learning to 'flow where he is directed' the Sufi becomes a means by which the will of God can be enacted with a minimum of interference. As in the story of a girl's first violin lesson, when the teacher said, 'Here is the violin, and here is the bow, now don't get in the way,' the Sufi tries to 'keep out of the way', so that the music of his Beloved can be clearly heard.

The goal of the Sufi training is to lead a guided life and to be in a state of continual absorption, merged within the One. This is the work of a lifetime, taking thirty to forty years. It is a gradual process. But the first step towards this state is the surrender to the will of the Teacher:

> A complete surrender to the Teacher is the first step leading to complete surrender to the Will of God. Only little by little can we get used to this idea. It must be absorbed, become part and parcel of the blood, just as food is absorbed into the body and becomes part of it. It must be integrated as a Wholeness into the mind. This is the Goal of the Spiritual Teaching.[8]

The function of the Sufi Shaikh is to help the disciple grow towards the Goal, and yet the Shaikh does not teach anything, but rather his 'state of being' influences the disciple. 'It is the spirit which quickens', wrote St Paul, and the spiritual vibrations of the Teacher 'speed up' the disciple, just as a faster horse will quicken a slower horse, or a more powerful electric current will effect a less powerful current. Empty, and merged in the emptiness, 'so totally absorbed in God that he no longer has any existence of his own',[9] the Shaikh reflects both the aspirations and the blemishes of the disciple, who can then more clearly see the direction of his quest, and the work that needs to be done. The Shaikh himself is nothing, but an empty space within which the seeker can realise his aspirations, as is imaged in the following dream, in which the Teacher is a shopkeeper:

> I enter a shop and the Teacher is behind the counter, though she doesn't seem to be selling anything. I have a desire for an amethyst ring that my grandmother gave me and I had lost; then I see an amethyst ring on my finger, engraved with the initial 'B', my mother's initial. Then the Teacher brings out a drawer full of amethysts of all different shapes and sizes. Although she doesn't ask for money or anything I know that this is a shop, and that the things are not free. It is important what one chooses. Then a man comes in smoking a pipe, filling the shop with smoke. I am horrified as the Teacher in real life doesn't like people smoking, but then I look and see that she is smoking also.

Central to this dream is the image of the Teacher as a mirror, reflecting first the desire of the dreamer for an amethyst ring, and then the smoking of the man. This can be read as the Teacher reflecting both the positive and negative qualities within the Wayfarer; and indeed, as the devil often appears in a cloud of smoke, the man 'smoking a pipe' suggests the archetype of evil. On a human level the Teacher will have likes and dislikes, and moreover shun evil in favour of good (in fact the ethics of this Path are very high: to possess something that one does not use is regarded as theft, and one must never hurt another's feelings); and yet at the same time nothing is rejected, for everything is a part of Him, and the Saint, being one with Him, is Everything. There is a story about one of the Superiors of this Line, Jami, who, drunk with love, was wandering in the street after curfew-time. A young soldier of the watch stopped him and asked, 'Are you a thief?' To which Jami replied 'I am.' So Jami was arrested and put in the cells for the night. When next morning the officer came to the cells he was horrified to discover that the great saint of the town had been arrested. Asking the soldier what had happened, the soldier said that the man admitted to being a thief. The officer asked Jami if this was so, to which Jami replied, 'What am I not?'

Thus everything is embraced, everything is accepted, even Satan himself. In fact the Sufi says 'Make the devil your friend', just as in a dream told earlier[10] the dreamer on the tightrope took the 'fork' from the shadow figure, and used it as a balancing pole. It is through the help of the shadow that, confronted with one's own inner darkness, one learns the lesson of humility; and while a friend will not tell you your faults, an enemy will:

> If somebody speaks ill of you, give him the place of honour in your courtyard; for he will be the cause of you being able to better yourself. A friend will not tell you the truth, but an enemy will . . .[11]

This dream also images the process by which the Teacher 'gives the seeker what he wants'. When the dreamer enters the shop she (the dreamer is a woman) 'has a desire for an amethyst ring that my grandmother gave me and I had lost', and an amethyst ring, with her mother's initial, then appears on her finger. Psychologically, the amethyst ring which the dreamer had lost suggests her true feminine identity, for rings are a symbol of wholeness; and as the grandmother usually represents the archetypal realm, this femininity has its origins in the very depths of the psyche. Living in the world today, it is easy for a woman to lose contact with her own deep feminine identity, which must be reclaimed from the unconscious. The amethyst ring 'engraved with the initial "B", my mother's initial', could indicate that one way for the dreamer to realise her feminine self is through her mother, or what her mother represents for her. The first impression of the feminine comes from the mother, and the true archetypal nature of the feminine is therefore 'stamped' or 'engraved' by the mother. In particular, the experience of the feminine archetype is affected by the mother's relationship to her own femininity, and her relationship to her daughter. Thus, finding on her finger the amethyst ring engraved with her mother's initial, the dreamer can begin to rediscover her own true feminine self.

As the spiritual Path is a journey towards wholeness, the dreamer needs to rediscover that which has been lost, and possibly the amethyst on her finger had always been there,

but only made visible by the presence of the Teacher. The
Teacher does nothing but help reveal what we have always
possessed, only failed to notice or kept hidden. In the
presence of the Teacher not only is the Wayfarer faced with
his inner darkness, but also his inner jewels are revealed to
him. And this happens through the Teacher simply accepting
and loving the seeker as he is. For, as I have already
mentioned, the Teacher does not judge or reject, as the world
does; rather he understands why the human being is as he is:
why there is the darkness and why there is the light. This
acceptance by the Teacher of the whole of the human being
has the effect of allowing that which has been hidden or
repressed to come to the surface, to be loved and so transformed.

Yet the dreamer's desire for an amethyst is not only
answered by her seeing the ring on her finger, but also by
the Teacher showing her 'a drawer full of amethysts of all
different shapes and sizes'. It is as if the dreamer is shown
many different aspects of the same situation, many forms of
the same jewel that is her feminine self, and at the same time
she is presented with a choice. And interestingly, the dreamer
knows that although the Teacher does not ask for money or
anything, it is a shop and 'the things are not free'. She realises
it is important what one chooses. In spiritual life one must
pay, not with money, for a real Teacher will never ask for
money – like the sunshine he is for the rich and the poor alike
– but with self-discipline, devotion, aspiration and inner
work. And if one wants the Absolute Truth, one must pay
with oneself; the ego must be sacrificed.

The Teacher is there to give the seeker what he wants, and
not everybody wants the Truth. Few are prepared to pay that
price, for 'who wants to get rid of the little self?' Many are
content with making just a few more steps towards the Goal:

> People want different things; they are after different things.
> They get it. Never more than what they want.[12]

Therefore, at the very core of this dream is the important
question of choice. The dreamer must choose what she
wants, whether to ask for a lost ring, and thus make an
important psychological step, or whether to ask for total

annihilation in the Nothingness. A ninth-century Sufi, Abmad Bin Khazrivia, had a dream about his contemporary, Abū Yazīd al-Bīstāmī, one of our spiritual ancestors;[13] in this dream Bin Khazrivia had a vision of God, and God said to him, 'Everybody desires something from Me but Abū Yazīd; he always asks only for Myself.'[14] When Abū Yazīd was asked by his followers, 'What is the proper task of true men?' he replied, 'The true man attaches his heart to none but God.'[15] If the Wayfarer has the desire together with the perseverance for this one 'true task', he is able to follow, however humbly, in the footsteps of such Saints, and the Naqshbandi System, the Path of the Masters, will take him along the Royal Road to God.

10

THE INVISIBLE BRIDEGROOM

The heart alone knows what the substance of love is,
The eye of reason has no power to behold it.

(Anon.)

I dream that I am looking into a mirror and I see my face.
Suddenly I realize that my eyes have changed. They look different. They somehow look larger and the colour is greenish with
a tinge of gold or gold with a tinge of green. They seem like
deep pools of stillness and peace filled with a kind of liquid light.
They are not my eyes and yet they are my eyes. But I know it
is not me who is looking through them. A strange and beautiful
feeling. It is as if He is looking through my eyes. Strange . . .

I change the expression of my face and put on this radiant
smile, which usually changes the expression of my eyes and
gives them a piercing spark. My face took on this expression yet
the eyes are as still and peaceful as before. They are not touched
by the grimace of the face, which makes it look rather empty
and false. The eyes are true.

The Sufi path is a mysterious journey into the Heart of
Hearts, that secret centre of the heart where the Beloved
meets the lover. There, in this inner sanctum, a transformation happens to the very nature of the lover; a transformation
which it is impossible to describe with words. However,
some dreams image different aspects or 'stages' of this
process. These dreams, which I will look at in this final
chapter, often have particular Sufi symbols, and can only be
understood in relationship to the Path of Love.

This dream about the dreamer's eyes describes such a
process of transformation. The eye is known as the 'mirror
of the soul', but here the dreamer sees that her eyes have

changed, and it is 'as if He is looking through my eyes'. This transformation of the dreamer's eyes images a mystical state in which the lover's soul becomes merged within the Beloved, and then He looks at the Beauty of His Creation through the eyes of the lover. *Fanā fi'llāh*, merging with God, is the last stage of the Path, and thus this dream has a prophetic nature, alluding to the *unio mystica* when the lover becomes one with the Beloved: 'I am he whom I love; he whom I love is me'.[1] This union is also reflected in the colour of the dreamer's eyes, 'greenish with a tinge of gold or gold with a tinge of green'; for, while the transformation into gold is the aim of the *opus*, green, as has been mentioned, is the colour of the Realisation of God.[2] The quality of her eyes 'like deep pools of stillness and peace, filled with a kind of liquid light' further suggests that they reflect Eternity, 'the still point of the turning world',[3] and they have a similarity to the eyes of the Sufi Master, Bhai Sahib, which Irina Tweedie describes when she first met him:

> Next moment he stood in front of me, quietly looking at me with a smile. He was tall, had a kindly face and strange eyes – dark pools of stillness they were, with a sort of liquid light in them, like golden sparks.[4]

These are the eyes of a Great Man, who is One with God, and the Path of the Wayfarer is first to merge with the Teacher, and then to merge with God.

What the dreamer sees in the mirror 'are not my eyes . . . and yet they are my eyes', and here lies the mystery of creation: that just as we are separate from Him and yet a part of Him, so He is separate from us and yet is the innermost part of our being: 'closer to you than yourself to yourself'.[5] In the Koran it is said that He is 'closer than our very neck vein'. In this dream the dreamer experiences this paradox, and He who is not other than her own Self looks through her eyes. Yet there is another profound metaphysical truth within this image, which is that through the *unio mystica* not only does the seeker come to know his Creator, but the Creator comes to know His Creation. When the eyes of the seeker are opened to God, so too are His Eyes opened, and in the mirror of the world He sees Himself. Thus, as the

Beloved unites with the lover, so He fulfils Himself, for 'I was hidden treasure, and I desired to be known, so I created the world.'

In the second part of the dream the dreamer changes the expression on her face into a grimace, and yet her eyes do not change as they usually do. 'They are not touched by the grimace of the face which makes it look rather empty and false. The eyes are true.' Whatever the outward expression of the dreamer, her eyes reflect the True Reality of the Heart. The Heart of the Beloved merges with the heart of the lover, and although the lover still lives in the outer world of appearances, within there is no such duality.

> I am moving all day
> And not moving at all.
> I am like the moon underneath
> The waves that ever go rolling.[6]

But what is it that makes a human being turn away from the world and begin the long and painful path Home? The spiritual quest is only a response to a Call, for just as you do not find a Teacher, but rather the Teacher finds you, attracted by the light of your aspiration, so God must first look upon man, before man looks for God. It is when the Eye of God looks upon the heart that the fire of longing is lit:

> Your eye shed the blood
>   of my heart,
> Then you said:
>   Keep it a secret.[7]

He decides to whom He would reveal Himself, to whom He would make His Secret known. And it is the Wine from His Eyes that so intoxicates the Sufi that this world becomes meaningless, 'Drunk and devastated by the Beloved's eye'.[8]

With a single kiss He poisons those whom He wants for Himself. Once one has been poisoned, branded by His kiss, then the pain of separation grows within the heart, and one gives anything, everything, life itself, for just another kiss:

> I would love to kiss you
> The price of kissing is your life

> Now my love is running toward my life,
> Shouting, 'What a bargain . . . let's buy it.'[9]

Here Rumi speaks the parts of the Beloved and the lover. The love awoken by a single kiss is enough to die for, for there is a secret about His kiss, it is not on the lips. When He kisses you it is on the *inside of the heart*. And He comes with such tenderness. He is just there, inside your heart, in infinite sweetness. In all human love affairs there is always duality, you and the one you love. Even when making love, in the most intimate moments, there are two. But when He loves you there is no duality. He is not separate from you, and He loves you from the inside. Can anyone resist such a kiss? All those who have tasted such wine become drunkards, and would ruin their whole life, give it away, for just another drink.

The image of drunkenness is used throughout Sufi litera-ture to refer to the state of intoxication with God, when all rational considerations are lost. On the worldly stage, being in love is often associated with a loss of reason, we talk of 'madly in love' or 'crazy with love'; how much more does the experience of Divine love overwhelm the mind:

> Drag me in chains, into the gang
>   of the insane, for the elation
> Of drunkenness to me
>   excels any sober consciousness.[10]

Yet in order to reach this state of drunkenness, this mystical absorption in love, the Wayfarer must free himself from the chains of the mind. This is clearly imaged in the following dream:

> I am in the audience of a theatre. A woman is giving out 'cards of destiny'. She throws a card to me. It is the Queen of Hearts.

In this dream, the Queen of Hearts alludes to the Path of Love as the dreamer's destiny. But there is a poignant association with the character of the Queen of Hearts in Lewis Carroll's *Alice in Wonderland*, who continually orders 'Off with their heads'. The dreamer must 'lose her head', abandon all of the constraints of the mind, if she is to progress on the Path. In Sufi literature the Path is imaged as a series of seven valleys.[11] The 'First Valley' is the 'Valley of the Quest', in which the seeker undergoes the painful process of turning away from the world and seriously entering upon the spiritual quest. In this valley everything that seemed precious must be given up, then the heart is filled with such longing that all that matters is the Goal. In this 'First Valley' the door to spiritual life is opened, but once the Wayfarer has passed through he comes to the 'Second Valley', 'The Valley of Love'. In the 'Valley of Love' reason must be abandoned:

> In this valley, love is represented by fire, and reason by smoke. When love comes reason disappears. Reason cannot live with the folly of love; love has nothing to do with human reason. If you possessed inner sight, the atoms of the visible world would be manifested to you. But if you look at things with the eye of ordinary reason you will never understand how necessary it is to love. Only a man who has been tested and is free can feel this. He who undertakes this journey should have a thousand hearts so that he can sacrifice one at every moment.[12]

To forsake 'reason' is not to be misinterpreted as encouraging an unbalanced way of life. As in the dream in which the Teacher's Guru showed a film of himself as a young man flying a kite,[13] in order to 'reach the heights' one must have both feet firmly on the ground – 'No hystericisms please, both feet firmly on the ground.' And one contemporary Sufi told his disciples, 'There are four important qualities needed for spiritual life. Common sense, aspiration and more common sense. The disciples then asked, 'What is the fourth quality?' To which he replied, 'Still more common sense!' The image of the dreamer having to 'lose her head' does not point towards mental instability, but rather to the fact that it is the continual workings of the mind that imprison us in this world of illusion, and therefore the mind is known as 'the slayer of the Real'. In the West we have become so conditioned to value the mind and its knowledge, that we have forgotten the knowledge of the heart. When Jung visited the Pueblos in New Mexico he talked to one of their chiefs, who commented on the white people, saying how cruel they looked, and how uneasy and restless they were.

His people thought they were mad. Jung asked the old man why he thought the whites were mad:

> 'They say that they think with their heads' he replied.
> 'Why of course. What do you think with?' I asked him in surprise.
> 'We think here,' he said, indicating his heart.[14]

THE WAYS OF LOVE

For the Sufi, the Real knowledge lies beyond the mind, in the heart. Therefore 'the mind must be hammered into the heart', for while the mind dwells in unreality, the heart is the home of Truth. The Path of Love takes the Wayfarer on a journey where the mind cannot follow, therefore as much as the ego must be surrendered, so must the mind:

> Kabir says: 'I tell you the ways of love! Even though the head itself must be given, why should you weep over it?'[15]

But in practice how is this achieved? How does the Sufi learn to surrender the mind, which is such a dominant part of our waking consciousness? The answer is through love, for love has a dynamic effect that actually 'drowns' the mind in the heart. And if worldly lovers are often not able to reason clearly, but are just absorbed in the object of their love, how much more is this so for those who make the King of Love their Goal? In the words of Rumi: 'Love is the sea where intellect drowns.'[16]

The ability of love to 'drown' the mind is an integral part of the Naqshbandi System. Irina Tweedie records how her Teacher actually 'switched off' her mind with his yogic powers:

> From time to time my Teacher switched off my mind, the result being that the mind would work to a quarter of its strength or half according as it was switched off, 25%, or 50% or sometimes even 75%. In the latter case one could hardly think. It was never done for a long time; one cannot live without the mind. It was done to help me so that the quality of the Higher Principle, the

spiritual insight, could come through, otherwise the mind clutters the channel of communication with its restless modifications. The state of mindlessness is quite painless and very peaceful; one just cannot think. That is all.[17]

As I have mentioned, Irina Tweedie was on the Path of *Tyaga*, while most Wayfarers are on the Path of *Dhyana* and are not subjected to such intense states. However, one of the effects of *Satsang* (sitting in the presence of the Teacher) is that the thinking function of the mind is slowed down, thus making the *Dhyana* meditation easier. *Dhyana* meditation, which is technically a state of yogic relaxation rather than meditation, is a method of focusing on the heart and the feeling quality of love within the heart; and as thoughts come into the mind you 'merge them within the feeling of love'. Eventually, and it can sometimes take years, the thinking process stops and you experience the state of *Dhyana*, the complete abstraction of the senses, in which the individual mind is thrown into the Universal Mind. At first this state can seem like sleeping, and indeed people often complain that they are just sleeping rather than meditating. But gradually you begin to experience a state of being, and then one day you are aware that you are awake on another plane of consciousness. This is when the spiritual experiences really commence, in the states of *Samadhi*, or 'super consciousness'.

What actually happens during the *Dhyana* meditation is that the feeling of love spins the heart chakra, which in turn stills the mind. The less the mind interferes, the greater the feeling of love and so the faster the heart chakra spins. Thus this meditation works like a chain reaction, generating love and drowning the mind. Love is what takes the Wayfarer to God:

> The disciple progresses through love. Love is the driving force, the greatest power of creation. As the disciple has not enough love in him to have sufficient of the propelling power to reach the Goal, so love is increased, or 'created' simply by activating the heart chakra.[18]

The Naqshbandi System is 'the only Yoga System where love is created in this way,' and the only System in which God is 'realized in one life, in this life'.[19] This Path is a direct and simple Road to God, rejecting anything which does not take the seeker closer to the Truth, as is illustrated in the following story from *Daughter of Fire*:

> My Grandfather and the Guru of my Reverend Guru have learned that a great Saint had come to live in a town nearby. They went to him with the intention of staying there for ten days. After four days the Saint inquired from them why they came and what they wanted from him.
>
> 'We have learnt that you are a Great Man of our time,' they answered. 'And as we are without guidance, we would like to ask you for a sitting and we would like to stay with you.' After fifteen or twenty minutes the Saint said:
>
> 'If I direct my attention towards you, you won't be able to bear it. My look is so powerful that if I look at a stone, I split it in two.'
>
> They went out and searched for a stone, the largest they could carry, and brought back such a heavy one that they could only carry it with difficulty. It was put before the Saint. He looked at the stone, and with one glance it was split in two. The Grandfather made a deep bow.
>
> 'Sir,' he said, 'we have met a juggler and a magician under the disguise of a Saint.'
>
> 'Why do you speak like this?' said the Saint obviously displeased. 'People say that I am a Great Man.'
>
> 'Surely you are a great man; it takes great power to do such a deed. But with all your power you cannot split a human heart. We are simple people. But we can turn the heart of a human being so that the human being will go on and on, where nobody can even imagine it.'
>
> And so they left.[20]

Sufis are simple people living ordinary lives, working, raising families and at the same time trying to reach Reality. And this is true as much for the Teacher as for his disciples, as is suggested by the following dream:

> I walked down an ordinary street and knocked on the door of an ordinary house and the Teacher opened the door.

Spiritual life is nothing extraordinary, it is just realising one's own inner essence; as Mother Theresa comments: 'Holiness is not the luxury of the few, holiness is a simple Duty for

you and me. We have been created for that.' Thus the Sufi
Masters have always lived simple lives. Yūsuf Hamadānī, the
first of the *Khwajagan*, or Masters of Wisdom,[21] lived a life
of poverty, always supporting himself and his family by his
own work. And this tradition continues to the present, with
Sufis never exhibiting the outer show or glamour that is
often associated with an Eastern Guru. Irina Tweedie's
Teacher was a householder with a large family; the green-
grocer who lived at the end of his street did not even know
that he was a Guru.

The simplicity of this Path of Love is reflected in the
imagery of the next dream, which has a hidden botanical
symbolism:

> First I saw bees and a beehive. Then I saw a flowering foxglove,
> perfect as only nature can make things perfect. The petals were
> a perfect subtle golden yellow. The quality was so delicate it was
> breathtaking.

The colour of the Naqshbandiyya-Mujaddidiya Order of
Sufism is golden yellow, and they are called the 'Golden
Sufis' or 'Silent Sufis' because they practise silent meditation.
Therefore, this image of the golden yellow flowering foxglove symbolises this Sufi System; and just as the Way of the
Tao is the Way of Nature, so too this feminine Path to God
is in harmony with the deepest rhythms of life, allowing the
flowering of the soul to take place, 'as the flower grows,
unconsciously'. Here Sufism echoes the ancient wisdom of
the alchemists, who said:

> you should employ venerable Nature, because from her and
> through her is our art born and in naught else: and so our
> magisterium is the work of Nature and not of the worker.[22]

In this dream, what is revealed is 'perfect as only nature can
make things perfect'.

However, the foxglove has a particular symbolism in that
the extract of its leaves produces the heart drug, digitalis.
This drug was used as a poison, seeming to create a heart
attack, but it is also used for healing purposes. Apparently
the leaves of the plant contain a number of alkaloids that

effect the heart muscles. What is significant to this dream is
the association of the golden yellow flowers with the heart,
for this Sufi System works through the heart chakra:

> In our Yoga System the ultimate result is achieved in one life by
> Dhyana. Only one Chakra is awakened: the Heart Chakra. It is
> the only Yoga School, in existence, in which love is created by
> the spiritual Teacher. It is done with Yogic Power. The result
> is, that the whole work of the awakening, of quickening, is done
> by one Chakra, which gradually opens up all the others. This
> Chakra is the Leader, and the Leader is doing everything. If you
> want to buy a part of my property, do you go to the property?
> Certainly not, you come to me. You deal with the proprietor.
> And in our System we deal only with the Leader.[23]

In this Path of Love the heart is the King, for the Beloved is
to be found there, in the very centre, in the Heart of Hearts:

> When the fragrance of the I am He is upon the wind,
> The bee of the heart finds the flower of its choice,
> And nestles there, caring for no other thing.[24]

From the essence of the flower the bee makes its honey,
and honey has always had a spiritual symbolism: it is a food
of the Gods, and for the Christians, 'the sweetness of the
divine word'.[25] For the Sufi, honey is the sweetness of the
soul melting in the Heart of the Beloved:

> Open the window to the west, and be lost in the sky of love;
> Drink the sweet honey that steeps the petals of the lotus of
>   the heart.[26]

For as much as the beginning of the Road is hard and stony,
so the end is the bliss of annihilation in love:

> I drained this cup;
> there is nothing now,
> but ecstatic annihilation.[27]

At first the ego dies on the cross of suffering, but the final
death is sweet, as is beautifully imaged in the following
dream, which puzzled the dreamer for some time:

> I dream that I have been sentenced to death by some business

men. I await to hear the type of death to which I have been sentenced. They come and tell me that I am to be drowned in honey.

The Path of Love leads the Wayfarer beyond the mind, into the bliss that awaits us in the heart. But first the heart must be empty of the ego, otherwise there is no space for Him. Rumi tells the story of a man who knocks at a door.

'Who's there?' asked a voice from within.
  'It's me,' says the man.
  'Go away then,' answers the voice. 'There's no room here for "me".'
  The man goes away and wanders in the desert until he realizes his error. He returns and knocks again at the door.
  'Who's there?' asks the voice.
  'Thou,' answers the man.
  'Then come in,' the voice replies.

And how does the ego go? It goes with much suffering, with sorrow and tears. That is why on this Sufi Path there will never be many. Bhai Sahib said, 'We will never be many, for who wants to get rid of the little self?' But that is the only way to reach the infinite ocean of bliss which is the home of the soul. In the words of a Sufi, Ansari of Herat:

Know that when you learn to lose yourself, you will reach the Beloved. There is no other secret to be learnt, and more than that is not known to me.

If you really love someone, they are all that matters. You think of that person all day long. If you are in love it can be like a madness; nothing else is important. You cease to exist, only the beloved exists. This can happen with a human love, and how much more can it happen with the Divine Lover. This is why Sufis are called 'Fools of God'; they are mad with their love for Him. In the story of Layla and Majnun, Majnun went mad because of his love for Layla, and he said, 'One name is better than two. If you knew what it means to be a lover, you would realize that one only has to scratch him and out falls the beloved.'
On the Path of Love the longing of the heart drives the

Wayfarer to such despair that he becomes like Majnun, and the Beloved is all that exists for him. Nothing else matters, nothing else has any importance. This has happened to Sufis over the centuries, and it continues to happen today, though until now little has been described in writing, except in Persian love poetry.[28] The Sufi Path is alive, and seekers are 'cooked' in the traditional way: the ego is ground down until little remains. When Irina Tweedie returned to London after being with Bhai Sahib, people knew that she had been with a Sufi Master, and asked it what it was like. She replied, 'It was like being run over by a steamroller.'

But finally, the ego cannot transcend itself. However much one works upon oneself, the last stage is always an act of grace. The ninth-century Sufi, al-Tirmidhī, tells a story which illustrates this.[29] He describes the whole situation as a man who is trying to uproot a tree:

There is a man who one day awakens to the idea that he has an ego, that he has the *nafs*, and that these *nafs* are in the way. He realises that if he is to reach the Truth he has to get rid of them, so what does he do? He does all sorts of practices in order to get rid of the 'branches of the tree'. The tree has many branches. The branches are really attachments, possessions; for it is through the ego that we have attachments, whether material attachments, or being attached to a job or position in society. So the man starts cutting the branches of the tree. He is going to cut all his ties, the bonds that imprison him. Perhaps he sells his house, and goes wandering in the desert with a bag on his shoulders. Some of these Sufis were also theologians, and had a seat somewhere in the mosque. So he leaves his seat. Then everything feels fine, and he is sure that he is on the right path, until he awakens one day and sees 'Hey, the trunk is here . . . I've cut the branches of the tree but the trunk is still here.' So he says to himself, 'Now I'm going to cut the trunk.' This image suggests that he is going to cut all the basic things that connect him with the earth. He wears only rags and he starts fasting. He goes about with a begging bowl and eats only the things that people throw to him. Now he is sure that he has cut the trunk of the tree. The branches are not there and what remains of the tree withers and apparently dies. So the ego seems to have gone, the *nafs* has been conquered.

But then one day our Wayfarer sees little shoots coming out of the trunk of the tree. The ego is still there. What is more, he has started to have spiritual experiences, and these experiences are so powerful that he overlooks the ego, which in all its cunning finds a way to infiltrate again and proclaim, 'I had a spiritual experience. This experience belongs to me.' The man then becomes full of despair, for he realises that the *nafs* is everywhere. As long as he exists within his body, and has a certain personality and character, he can't escape the devilish tricks of the *nafs*. He has exhausted all his efforts and found that the ego is still alive and well. He then becomes hopeless and helpless. There is nothing to go back to, for he has left the world behind, but there is no possibility to go forward. Loneliness, darkness, bewilderment and deep fatigue are his lot. Wherever he turns, he finds his ego. All his efforts are in vain, and so all his efforts subside.

The man then calls out in his despair and says, 'How can I avoid my lower self from the sweetness of these spiritual experiences? I can do this no more than white hair can turn black. I have harnessed my lower self with true submission to God, but my self broke off and went loose. And how shall I catch it again?' And he sinks into a desert of bewilderment, lonely and desolate. No longer close to himself . . . and not yet close to God. Then, from the depths of his despair he cries out to God, 'You who know all the hidden things. You know that there is not even one step left for me in the realm of true efforts. And that it is not possible for me to wipe away the lusts and desires from my self, from my heart. I plead with Thee then, save me, rescue me.' The compassion of God reaches him and he is blessed. And from the stage where he had stopped his heart is lifted in a flash to the stage of proximity. There he breathes the breath of Divine Proximity and in its space he expands.

In this story al-Tirmidhī describes how there comes the time when the Wayfarer feels that he can go no further, but can only wait and wait, his heart burning with longing. For it is one of the mysteries of the Path that the lover, being imperfect, cannot merge into God, but must always wait for He, who is perfect, to 'merge into the soul': 'It is a strange thing with Love, that it is the Beloved who merges into the lover.'[30] When He wills, He comes. It is only then that the ego goes, when the lover disappears in the Beloved's embrace:

> Love came
>   flowed like blood
>   beneath the skin, through veins
> emptied me of my self
>   filled me with the Beloved
> till every organ was seized
>   and occupied
> till only
>   my name remains
>   the rest is It.[31]

This is an experience of oneness with love. But who is the experiencer when the ego is not there? Bhai Sahib told Irina Tweedie that people would ask him, 'Have you realized God? Have you realized the Self?' and he would answer, 'I have not realized God, I have not realized the Self.' When he said this Irina Tweedie laughed, 'Bhai Sahib, this is a lie! It is not nice to tell a lie!' But he replied, 'Why a lie? If I am nowhere how can I realize something? To realize something there must be somebody to realize: if I am nothing, if I am nowhere, how can I have realized something?'[32]

The sweet taste of honey, the draught of wine, these are the Beloved's gifts, given to one who has waited with longing and perseverance. For before the lover can receive such bounty his heart must be pure and empty; and yet in the niche of the heart the pure gold chalice has always stood, waiting . . .

> A woman who often symbolizes my Higher Self reached into a little shrine set back in the wall and covered with a blue cloth. She brought out a small golden chalice.

In this dream it is the Higher Self of the dreamer who reveals her own pure Self, 'a small golden chalice'. This chalice had always been there, kept in a small shrine, but now the time is right for the dreamer, who is a woman, to be given this chalice. The chalice is an ancient symbol, associated in Christianity with the Last Supper and the Legend of the Grail. At the Last Supper Christ gave his disciples a cup of wine to drink:

And he said unto them, this is my blood of the new testament, which is shed for many.[33]

And there is a legend that in this same cup Joseph of Arimathea caught the blood of Christ on the cross. For Christians, the blood of Christ, symbolically drunk at communion, is the life of the spirit, and the chalice is therefore the purity of heart needed to live a life of the spirit. For the Sufi, the chalice is associated with the heart and when filled with the wine of the Beloved it symbolises 'the knowledge of God' which is 'granted purely through Divine Grace, for "it is the Grace of God, granted to whomever He wills"' (Koran III, 73).[34] Thus the golden chalice symbolises the purity of heart which is ready to receive His wine, and thus come to know Him.

Through her aspirations and inner-work, the dreamer has reached the stage where she is able to see the treasure that has been hidden in the shrine of her heart. And this treasure is the empty cup in which He can reveal Himself. The shrine itself is covered by a blue cloth, and blue is the colour of the feminine and of devotion. As I have mentioned this Sufi Path is a feminine, devotional Path; but as the dreamer is a woman the blue cloth could also suggest that the chalice is hidden within her own feminine self. Each of us, in the depths of ourselves, have such a chalice, but it is not given to us until we are ready; for we cannot drink His wine until our heart is turned towards Him. We cannot come to see His face until we have left the world far behind, and are surrendered to Him.

To be constantly surrendered to God, to be His slave and to long for nothing but union with Him, this is the aim of the Sufi. In this final dream, the dreamer stands alone at the altar rail, bound hand and foot:

> I am going to get married, a proper marriage. I am dressed in white and everything is beautiful and fine as one would imagine it. The only thing is that there is no bridegroom. I am walking on my own down the aisle and I see that my whole family and my background are sitting in the church pretending that it is a normal wedding taking place. Then I come to the altar and the priest is waiting for me. A little ceremony takes place, the exchange of rings, but the priest puts one ring around both

wrists and one around both ankles. Then he leans me against the cross and I am faced towards the aisle and then they (my family etc.) all leave, because they cannot take the situation of me being there like that.

This was dreamt three times by the dreamer, and according to an esoteric tradition, if something is told three times it must be true.[35]

The dream images the mystical marriage, for the invisible bridegroom is the Beloved, and it is, indeed, a 'proper marriage'. But in the ceremony the ring, which is a token of this marriage, binds the bride as a slave. In the dream of the woman walking on a tightrope',[36] 'a gold ring around my left foot' imaged the dreamer as a slave of God, but here at the altar the rings more explicitly portray the slavery of the dreamer, who can no longer move of her own free will. Bound hand and foot, she is then leant against the cross, symbolising the crucifixion that will take her to God. On the cross the ego will die; this is the arena for those committed to the Path. And at this point the family and background of the dreamer 'all leave because they cannot take the situation of me being there like that', for they represent the conditioning and worldly ties of the dreamer, which must fall away in order to leave the soul free to go to God. But significantly it is they who leave the dreamer once she is married and on the cross, for on the Sufi Path it is the aspiration and commitment of the disciple that effects the process of psychological change. Just as the simple meditation of the heart activates the psyche and catalyses the process of alchemical transformation, so too, in the very practice of surrender do the worldly attachments, both physical and psychological, fall away, leaving an empty cup waiting to be filled with the wine of the Beloved:

> I offer to Thee the only thing I have,
> My capacity of being filled with Thee.

NOTES

INTRODUCTION

1. Maya Angelou, ITV television, 1988.
2. James Hillman, *Insearch*, p. 63.
3. Irina Tweedie, *Daughter of Fire*, p. 453.
4. J. C. Cooper, *An Illustrated Encylopedia of Traditional Symbols*, p. 40.

CHAPTER ONE

1. Irina Tweedie, *Daughter of Fire*, pp. 382–3.
2. See below, p. 9.
3. Idries Shah, *The Way of the Sufi*, p. 155.
4. Abu'l Qasim Qushayri, *Al-Risalatu'l-Qushayriyya Fi 'Ilmi'l-Tasawwue*, pp. 607–8.
5. *Al-Anwar al-Kudsiva* (The Divine Lights of the Naqshbandi Path) trans. Sara Sviri. See also Hasan Shushud, *The Masters of Wisdom of Central Asia*, p. 44.
6. al-Tirmidhī, *Bad'u al-Sha'n* (The Beginning of My Story).
7. Hafez, quoted by J. Nurbakhsh, *Sufi Symbolism*, Vol. 1, p. 149.
8. Quoted by Annemarie Schimmel, *Mystical Dimensions of Islam*, p. 225.
9. Irina Tweedie, *Daughter of Fire*, p. 12.
10. Ibid., p. 157.
11. Ibid., p. 113.
12. Irina Tweedie, 'Spiritual Sufi Training is a Process of Individuation Leading into the Infinite'. To be included in the forthcoming *Islam, Sufism and Jungian Psychology*, ed. M. Spiegleman.
13. Irina Tweedie, *Daughter of Fire*, pp. 321–5.
14. Ibid. pp. 65–6.
15. See below, p. 85.

16. Irina Tweedie, *Daughter of Fire*, p. 585.
17. See below, p. 121.
18. Irina Tweedie, *Daughter of Fire*, p. 345.

CHAPTER TWO

1. Irina Tweedie, *Daughter of Fire*, p. x.
2. C. G. Jung, *Memories, Dreams, Reflections*, p. 225.
3. Sara Sviri, 'Between Fear and Hope. On the Coincidence of Opposites in Islamic Mysticism', *Jerusalem Studies for Arabic and Islam*, 9, 1987, p. 327.
4. C. G. Jung *Collected Works* (hereafter referred to as *C.W.*) *Vol. 14 Mysterium Coniunctionis*, para. 296.
5. C. G. Jung, *C.W. 5*, para. 203.
6. E. Neumann, *The Great Mother*, p. 42.
7. Shakespeare, *Hamlet*, V ii 10–11.
8. 'Individuation' is fundamentally a natural developmental 'process immanent in every living organism' (Jolande Jacobi, *The Way of Individuation*, p. 15). It is what makes an acorn develop into an oak, a kitten turn into a cat. Within a human being it can occur 'more or less autonomously without the participation of consciousness'. But the more common understanding of the term is when it refers to an 'artificial' process, which is 'developed by definite methods' (for example analysis) and *'experienced consciously'*.
9. C. G. Jung, *The Psychology of the Transference*, p. 34.
10. *The Gospel according to St Matthew*, King James Version, 22: 34–5.
11. Marie-Louise von Franz, *C. G. Jung, His Myth in Our Time*, p. 227.
12. M. Nicoll, *Psychological Commentaries on the Teaching of Gurdjieff and Ouspensky*, Vol. I, p. 329.
13. Goso, quoted by Paul Reps, *Zen Flesh, Zen Bones*, p. 122.
14. R. Tagore, unidentified source.
15. Jolande Jacobi, *The Way of Individuation*, p. 107.
16. Ibid. pp. 108–9.
17. Irina Tweedie, *Daughter of Fire*, p. 132.
18. C. G. Jung, *Memories, Dreams, Reflections* p. 214.
19. C. G. Jung, *Collected Letters Vol. 2*, p. 195.
20. Irina Tweedie, *Daughter of Fire*, p. 226.
21. C. G. Jung, 'Commentary on Kundaline Yoga', *Spring* 1976, p. 176.

22. Individuals are born with two of the four functions more highly developed and accessible to consciousness. During the individuation process the individual aims to develop the use of the less evolved functions.
23. Irina Tweedie, *Daughter of Fire*, p. 221.

CHAPTER THREE

1. Irina Tweedie, *Daughter of Fire*, p. 268.
2. Ibid., p. 245. Rumi says something very similar: 'Soul receives from soul that knowledge, therefore not by book nor from tongue/If knowledge of mysteries comes after emptiness of mind, that is illumination of heart. (*Mathnawi* I, quoted by A. Reza Arasteh, *Rumi, The Persian, The Sufi*, p. 124.)
3. Yashuichi Awakawa, *Zen Painting*, pp. 125 and 126.
4. C. G. Jung, *C.W. 12*, plate 132.
5. For a fuller exploration of the function of the animus in relation to the woman's psyche, see below p. 54f.
6. For a fuller discussion of the feminine nature of this Sufi Path, and how it 'takes place through the unconscious', see below p. 69f. and 72f.
7. Irina Tweedie, unpublished interview, August 1988.
8. M. Spiegleman, *Buddhism and Jungian Psychology*, p. 55.
9. Ibid., p. 79.
10. Plato, *The Republic*, Book 7, Part 7.
11. C. G. Jung, *C.W. 5*, para. 497.
12. Quoted by Henry Corbin, *The Man of Light in Iranian Sufism*, p. 17.
13. C. G. Jung, *C.W. 11*, paras 58 and 60.
14. J. C. Cooper, *An Illustrated Encyclopedia of Traditional Symbols*, p. 71.
15. C. G. Jung, *C.W. 7*, para. 152.
16. Jung writes: 'Every psychic process has a value quality attached to it, namely its feeling tone. This indicates the degree to which the subject is "affected" by the process and how much it means to him (in so far as it reaches consciousness at all). It is through the affect that the subject becomes involved and so comes to feel the whole weight of reality. The difference amounts roughly to that between a severe illness that one reads about in a text book and a real illness which one has.' (*C.W. 9ii*, para. 61.)
17. The 'shadow' belongs to the unconscious, and thus can never be fully integrated into consciousness.

18. C. G. Jung, *C.W. 14*, para. 32.
19. Many ancient fertility festivals and customs relating to the Earth Mother were suppressed by the Church. For example, in England the Puritans banned the May Pole festival, supposedly because of the orgiastic behaviour that accompanied it.
20. C. G. Jung, *C.W. 12*, para. 299.
21. Ibid., para. 141.
22. Sohravardī, quoted by Henry Corbin, *The Man of Light in Iranian Sufism*, p. 21.
23. Irina Tweedie, *Daughter of Fire*, p. 350.
24. Quoted by Henry Corbin, *The Man of Light*, p. 77.

CHAPTER FOUR

1. See below, p. 91f.
2. *The Hermetic Museum*, 1:13, trans. Waite, quoted E. Edinger, *Anatomy of the Psyche*, p. 11.
3. Marie-Louise von Franz, *C. G. Jung, His Myth in our Time*, p. 222.
4. C. G. Jung, *C.W. 12*, para. 433.
5. See above, p. 30f.
6. Irina Tweedie, *Daughter of Fire*, p. 345.
7. C. G. Jung, *C. G. Jung Speaking*, p. 229, quoted by E. Edinger, *Anatomy of the Psyche*, p. 147.
8. Jami, *Yusuf and Zulaikha*, trans. David Pendlebury, p. 61.
9. Rumi, 'Beware of Hurting the Saint', trans. R. A. Nicholson, *Rumi, Poet and Mystic*, p. 87.
10. Attar, *The Conference of the Birds*, trans C. S. Nott, p. 132.
11. C. G. Jung, *C. G. Jung, Emma Jung and Toni Wolff, A Collection of Remembrances*, p. 52.
12. See above Ch. 2, note 8.
13. Sallie Nichols, *Jung and Tarot*, Ch. 19.
14. C. G. Jung, *C.W. 5*, para. 235n.
15. Avicenna, 'Aquarium sap.', *Museum Hermeticum*, p. 85, quoted by Jung, *C.W. 13*, para. 263.
16. 'The Spirit Mercurius', *C.W. 13*, para. 239ff.
17. *C. G. Jung, Emma Jung and Toni Wolff, A Collection of Remembrances*, p. 75.
18. Idries Shah, *The Sufis*, p. 225.
19. St Augustine, *Confessions*, Lib. XIII, cap. XII, trans. F. J. Shield, p. 275, quoted by Jung, *C.W. 9ii*, para. 174.

CHAPTER FIVE

1. C. G. Jung, *C.W. 9ii*, para. 42.
2. C. G. Jung, *C.W. 12*, para. 219 and n.
3. Irene de Castillejo, *Knowing Woman*, p. 76.
4. Marie-Louise von Franz mentions four stages of development in both the animus and anima: first, the wholly physical man or woman – Tarzan, or Eve, the primitive, instinctual woman; second the romantic figure – Lord Byron or Helen of Troy; third, the animus is the bearer of the 'word' – a professor or clergyman, while the anima is a figure of spiritual devotion – the Virgin Mary; and fourth, the animus and anima as figures of wisdom – Ghandi or the Greek goddess of wisdom, Athena. *Man and His Symbols* pp. 184 and 195.
5. Marie-Louise von Franz, *Man and His Symbols* (ed. C. G. Jung), p. 194.
6. C. G. Jung, *C.W. 14*, para. 654.
7. E. Neumann, 'The Psychological Stages of Feminine Development', *Spring*, 1957, p. 72.
8. C. G. Jung, *Word and Image*, p. 211.
9. *The Book of Common Prayer*.
10. *Holy Bible* (King James Version), *Romans* 13. 14.
11. Irina Tweedie, *Daughter of Fire*, pp. 364–5.
12. J. Campell, *The Hero with a Thousand Faces*, p. 39.
13. *The Gospel According to St Matthew* (King James Version) 5. 3.
14. J. G. Bennett, *The Masters of Wisdom*, pp. 146–7.
15. See above p. 27.
16. See below p. 104.
17. Irina Tweedie, *Daughter of Fire*, p. 466.
18. This was enacted in some tribal societies, when, at the age of puberty or before, the boy would leave the women's hut. In nineteenth-century England a similar dynamic could be seen in the upper-middle class custom of sending boys away to boarding school, while the girls would remain at home.

CHAPTER SIX

1. See above, p. 17.
2. T. S. Eliot, 'Little Gidding', 11. 239–42.
3. E. Neumann, *The Great Mother*, p. 183n. In China, while the Dragon represents the masculine, yang energy, the Tiger

represents the feminine, yin energy. C. G. Jung, *C.W. 14*, para. 403n.
4. M. Esther Harding, *Woman's Mysteries*, p. 103.
5. E. Neumann, 'On the Moon and Matriarchal Consciousness', *Spring* 1954, pp. 93 and 95.
6. C. G. Jung, *C.W. 5*, para. 24.
7. A. Stevens, *Archetypes*, p. 265. The two hemispheres of the brain are joined by the *corpus callosum* which is a bundle of nerve fibres. It is via the *corpus callosum* that the left hemisphere can repress or inhibit the right hemisphere.
8. See above p. 24.
9. Irina Tweedie, *Daughter of Fire*, p. 227.
10. For the following passage on Abu Hafs and the Sufis of Nishapur, I refer to Sara Sviri, 'The Naqshbandi Path', unpublished lecture, Schwarzee, 1988.
11. There is no monastic life as such in Islam; however there were places like ashrams of monasteries in which dervishes could spend a certain amount of time.
12. See above p. 3.
13. Irina Tweedie, *Daughter of Fire*, p. 376.
14. Marie-Louise von Franz, *The Way of The Dream*, p. 167.

CHAPTER SEVEN

1. See above p. xii.
2. Irina Tweedie, *Daughter of Fire*, p. 95.
3. Ibid, pp. 158–9. The relationship between the surrender and the death of the ego is discussed in more detail below, p. 132–3.
4. C. G. Jung, recorded by Miguel Serrano, *C. G. Jung and Herman Hesse, A Record of Two Friendships*, p. 60.
5. See above p. 104.
6. Irina Tweedie, *Daughter of Fire*, p. 793.
7. Miguel Serrano, *C. G. Jung and Herman Hesse*, p. 60.

CHAPTER EIGHT

1. E. Edinger, *Anatomy of the Psyche*, p. 6.
2. Ibid., p. 6.
3. Maghrebi, trans. Javad Nurbakhsh, *Sufi Symbolism*, Vol. 1, p. 21.
4. C. G. Jung, *C.W. 9ii*, para. 231.
5. See above, p. 28.

6. See above, p. 72.
7. Nizami, *Layla and Majnun*, p. 126.
8. R. Tagore, *Fruit Gathering*, XXXVII (*Collected Poems and Plays*, pp.187–8).
9. Lao Tsu, *Tao Te Ching* (Trans. Gia-Fu Feng and Jane English), Chap. 46.
10. A. Samuels, *A Critical Dictionary of Jungian Analysis*, p. 150.
11. Lao Tsu, *Tao Te Ching*, Chap. 1.
12. C. G. Jung, *C.W. 9i* para. 646.
13. That the Self exists 'outside' the human psyche is reflected in a dream of Jung's in which he saw the Self imaged as a Yogi sitting in deep meditation in a roadside chapel. Looking closely at the face of the Yogi Jung realised that he had his face. 'I started in profound fright, and awoke with the thought: "Aha, so he is the one who is meditating me. He has a dream, and I am it." ' (*Memories, Dreams, Reflections*, p. 355.)
14. *Isha Upanishad*, 4–5, quoted by C. G. Jung, *C.W. 6*, para. 329.
15. Lahiji, quoted by Henry Corbin, *The Man of Light in Iranian Sufism*, p. 118.
16. Rumi, 'The Truth Within Us', *Rumi, Poet and Mystic*, trans. R. A. Nicholson, p. 47.
17. *The Revelation of St John the Divine* (King James Version), 21. 9–23.
18. Najmad-dīn Kubrā, quoted by Henry Corbin, *The Man of Light*, p. 72.

CHAPTER NINE

1. Rudyard Kipling, *If* quoted by Irina Tweedie, *Daughter of Fire*, p. 314.
2. C. G. Jung, *C.W. 8*, para. 759.
3. Ibid., para. 800.
4. Irina Tweedie, *Daughter of Fire*, p. 404.
5. Irina Tweedie, unpublished interview, summer 1988.
6. *The Revelation of St John the Divine* (King James Version), 22. 1.
7. Lao Tsu, *Tao Te Ching*, Ch. 48.
8. Irina Tweedie, *Daughter of Fire*, p. 133.
9. Lahiji, Commentary on *The Rose Garden of Mystery*, quoted by Henry Corbin *The Man of Light in Iranian Sufism*, p. 118.
10. See above, p. 24.
11. Irina Tweedie, *Daughter of Fire*, p. 340.
12. Ibid., p. 536.

13. See above p. 2.
14. Abu Al-Qasim Abdal Karim bin Hawalan Qaishri, *Risalah-i quashariyah (On Sufism)*.
15. Farid al-Din Attar, *Muslim Saints and Mystics*, p. 122.

CHAPTER TEN

1. Hallāj, quoted by Henry Corbin, *The Man of Light in Iranian Sufism*, p. 88.
2. See above p. 100.
3. T. S. Eliot 'Burnt Norton' 1. 62.
4. Irina Tweedie, *Daughter of Fire*, p. 5.
5. '*And He is with you*/with you/in your search/when you seek Him/look for Him/in your looking/closer to you/than yourself/to yourself'; from Rumi, 'A Thief in the Night' trans. Peter Lamborn Wilson and Nasrollah Pourjavady, *The Drunken Universe*, p. 105.
6. Zen poem, anon.
7. Attar, in J. Nurbakhsh, *Sufi Symbolism*, Vol. 1, p. 27.
8. Maghrebi, ibid. p. 27.
9. Rumi, *Open Secret*, trans. John Moyne and Coleman Barks, Quatrain 388.
10. Hafez, in J. Nurbakhsh *Sufi Symbolism*, p. 11.
11. See Attar, *The Conference of the Birds*, p. 98: 'The first valley is the Valley of the Quest, the second the Valley of Love, the third is the Valley of Understanding, the fourth is the Valley of Independence and Detachment, the fifth of Pure Unity, the sixth is the Valley of Astonishment, and the seventh is the Valley of Poverty and Nothingness beyond which one can go no further.'
12. Ibid., p. 102.
13. See above pp. 19–20.
14. C. G. Jung, *Memories, Dreams, Reflections*, p. 276.
15. Kabir, *Songs of Kabir*, (trans. R. Tagore), p. 141.
16. Rumi, trans. Daniel Liebert, *Rumi, Fragments, Ecstasies*, p. 64.
17. Irina Tweedie, 'Spiritual Sufi Training is a Process of Individuation Leading into the Infinite', unpublished paper.
18. Irina Tweedie, *Daughter of Fire*, p. 58.
19. Ibid., pp. 266–7.
20. Ibid., pp. 536–7.
21. See above, p. 2.
22. C. G. Jung, *The Psychology of the Transference*, p. 50.

23. Irina Tweedie, *Daughter of Fire*, p. 55.
24. Kabir, adapted from *Songs of Kabir*, p. 56.
25. J. C. Cooper, *An Illustrated Encyclopedia of Traditional Symbols*, p. 84.
26. Kabir, *Songs of Kabir*, p. 72.
27. Rumi, *Rumi, Fragments, Ecstasies*, p. 45.
28. In *Daughter of Fire*, Bhai Sahib tells Irina Tweedie that the experiences which she is having are 'not recorded anywhere except in Persian writings' (p. 268).
29. Sara Sviri, 'The Naqshbandi Path', unpublished lecture.
30. Irina Tweedie, *Daughter of Fire*, p. 407.
31. Abu Sa'id Abo'l-Khayr, 'Quatrain', trans. Peter Lamborn Wilson and Nasrollah Pourjavady *The Drunken Universe*, p. 101.
32. Irina Tweedie, *Daughter of Fire*, p. 558.
33. *The Gospel of St Mark* (King James Version) 14. 24.
34. Abo'l-Mofâkher Bâkhrazi, quoted by J. Nurbakhsh, *Sufi Symbolism*, Vol. 1, p. 138.
35. Similarly, if a question is asked three times it must be answered, as in the *Katha Upanishad*, when the boy Nachiketas meets the Spirit of Death, and asks to be taught the truth about death.
36. See above, p. 24.

SELECTED BIBLIOGRAPHY

Abu'l Qasim Qushayri. *Al-Risalatu'l-Qushayriyya Fi 'Ilmi'l-Tasawwue*, 1045–6.

al-Tirmidhī. *Bad'u al-Sha'n* (*The Beginning of My Story*) private trans.

Arasteh, A. Reza. *Rumi The Persian, The Sufi*, London: Routledge & Kegan Paul, 1974.

Attar, Farid ud-Din. *The Conference of the Birds*, trans. C. S. Nott, London: Routledge & Kegan Paul, 1961.

——*Muslim Saints and Mystics*, trans. A. J. Arberry, London: Routledge & Kegan Paul, 1966.

Awakawa, Yashuichi. *Zen Painting*, Tokyo: Kodansha International, 1970.

Bennett, J. G. *The Masters of Wisdom*, London: Turnstone Books, 1977.

Brother Lawrence, *The Practice of the Presence of God*, London: Samuel Badger and Sons.

Campell, Joseph. *The Hero with a Thousand Faces*, London: Abacus, 1975.

Castillejo, Irene de. *Knowing Woman*, New York: Harper Colophon, 1974.

Conrad, Joseph. *Heart of Darkness*, London: 1902.

Cooper, J. C. *An Illustrated Encyclopedia of Traditional Symbols*, London: Thames and Hudson, 1978.

Corbin, Henry. *Creative Imagination in the Sufism of Ibn 'Arabi*, Princeton: Princeton University Press, 1969.

——*The Man of Light in Iranian Sufism*, London: Shambala, 1978.

Edinger, Edward. *The Anatomy of the Psyche*, La Salle: Open Court, 1985.

Eliot, T. S. *Four Quartets*, London: Faber and Faber, 1944.

Franz, Marie-Louis von. *C.G. Jung, His Myth in Our Time*, New York: C. G. Jung Foundation, 1975.

——*The Way of the Dream*, Toronto: Windrose Films, 1988.

Harding, Esther. *Woman's Mysteries*, London: Rider, 1982.

Hesse, Herman. *Steppenwolf,* trans. Basil Creighton, Middlesex: Penguin, 1965.

Hillman, James. *Insearch: Psychology and Religion,* Dallas: Spring Publications, 1967.

Holy Bible, King James Version.

Jacobi, Jolande. *The Way of Individuation,* New York: Harcourt Brace and World, 1967.

Jami, *Yusuf and Zulaikha,* trans. David Pendlebury, London: Octagon Press, 1980.

Jensen, Ferne (ed.), *C. G. Jung, Emma Jung, Toni Wolff, A Collection of Remembrances,* San Francisco: The Analytical Psychology Club of San Francisco, 1982.

Jung, C. G. *Collected Works,* London: Routledge & Kegan Paul.

——*Psychology of the Transference,* London: Arc Paperbacks, 1983.

——*Memories, Dreams, Reflections,* London: Flamingo, 1983.

——*Collected Letters,* 2 Vols, London: Routledge & Kegan Paul, 1973 and 1976.

——*Word and Image,* Jaffe, Aniela (ed.), Princeton: Princeton University Press, 1979.

——*Man and His Symbols,* London: Aldus Books, 1964.

——'Commentary on Kundalini Yoga', *Spring,* 1975, pp. 1–33; and *Spring,* 1976, pp. 1–31.

Kabir, *Songs of Kabir,* trans. R. Tagore, New York: Samuel Weiser, 1977.

Neumann, Eric. *The Great Mother,* Princeton: Princeton University Press, 1963.

——'The Psychological Stages of Feminine Development', *Spring,* 1957, pp. 63–97.

Nicoll, Maurice, *Psychological Commentaries on the Teaching of Gurdjieff and Ouspensky,* London, Private printing by Kitchen and Barratt, 1949.

Nichols, Sallie. *Jung and Tarot, an Archetypal Journey,* Maine: Samuel Weiser, 1980.

Nizami, *The Story of Layla & Majnun,* trans. R. Gelpke, London: Bruno Cassirer, 1966.

Nurbakhsh, J. *Sufi Symbolism,* London: Khaniqahi-Nimatullahi Publications, 1984.

Plato. *The Republic,* trans. Desmond Lee, London: Penguin Books, 1955.

Reps, Paul. *Zen Flesh, Zen Bones,* Harmondsworth: Penguin Books, 1971.

Rumi, *Open Secret, Versions of Rumi,* trans. by John Moyne and Coleman Barks, Putney, Vermont: Threshold Books, 1984.

Rumi, *Rumi, Poet and Mystic*, trans. R. A. Nicholson, Northampton: John Dickens & Co., 1950.

Samuels, Andrew. *A Critical Dictionary of Jungian Analysis*, London: Routledge & Kegan Paul, 1986.

Serrano, Miguel. *C. G. Jung and Herman Hesse, A Record of Two Friendships*, London: Routledge & Kegan Paul, 1966.

Shah, Idries. *The Way of the Sufi*, London: Penguin Books, 1974.

——*The Sufis*, New York: Doubleday & Co., 1964.

——*Tales of the Dervishes*, London: Octagon Press, 1967.

Shakespeare, *Hamlet*, ed. Harold Jenkins, London: Methuen, 1982.

Shushud, Hasan. *Masters of Wisdom of Central Asia*, trans. Muhtar Holland, Ellingstring: Coombe Springs Press, 1983.

Spiegleman, Marvin. *Buddhism and Jungian Psychology*, Phoenix, Arizona: Falcon Press, 1985.

Sviri, Sara. 'Between Fear and Hope. On the Coincidence of Opposites in Islamic Mysticism', *Jerusalem Studies for Arabic and Islam*, 9, 1987, pp. 316–49.

Tagore, Rabindranath, *Collected Poems and Plays*, London: Macmillan, 1936.

Tweedie, Irina. *Daughter of Fire, A Diary of a Spiritual Training with A Sufi Master*, Nevada City: Blue Dolphin Publishing, 1986.

INDEX

THE CHASM OF FIRE

Irina Tweedie

Born in Russia in 1907, Irina Tweedie suffered the tragic loss of her husband in 1954. It was as a result of this experience - whilst searching for consolation and a meaning to life - that her journey of spiritual discovery began. Some five years later, her search took her to India - to the Sufi teacher who was to revolutionise her life. Written as a diary of her observations, this book is a detailed record of the author's spiritual training.

'It is an account of the slow grinding down of personality - a painful process, for man cannot remake himself without suffering. I had hoped to get instruction in yoga...but found myself forced to face the darkness within myself...I was beaten down in every sense till I had come to terms with that in me which I'd been rejecting all my life....'

It was only through this regeneration of herself that Irina Tweedie was able to taste the essence of True Liberation and know that *'the Path of Love is like a bridge of hair across a Chasm of Fire'*

208 pp   234 X 156 mm

£7.95

ISBN 1 85230 040 X

APOLLO VERSUS THE ECHOMAKER
Psychotherapy Dreams and Shamanism
A Laingian Approach

Anthony Lunt

R D Laing was the best known psychiatrist and psychoanalyst
of modern times, his work being both radical
and controversial.

In **Apollo Versus the Echomaker**, Anthony Lunt, who is
emerging as Laing's most prominent student, not only
challenges accepted views of psychotherapy and the meaning
of dreams, but also challenges you to understand yourself.
Cutting through the barriers of psychoanalytic theory, he
reaches into the heart of what it means to be human.

This is the first book of its kind on Laingian psychotherapy,
and includes extracts from Laing's previously unpublished
last interview.

*He brings to his work as a psychotherapist a sensitivity and
creativity, freedom from the spell of conventional theories, and an
independence of mind....* R D Laing, on the Author

128 pp 216 X 138mm

£6.95

ISBN 1 85230 153 8